# BLACK WOMEN LEADERS
## OF THE
# CIVIL RIGHTS MOVEMENT

### ZITA ALLEN

African American Experience
FRANKLIN WATTS
A *Division of Grolier Publishing*
New York / London / Hong Kong / Sydney
Danbury, Connecticut

*For My Mother*

---

*Chapter 1 opener: Gloria Richardson Dandridge and
U.S. Attorney General Robert Kennedy*

Book Design by Molly Heron
Photographs ©: AP/Wide World Photos: 46, 50, 55, 75; Archive
Photos: 88 (London Daily Express); Bettmann Archive: 20; New
York Public Library, Schomburg Center for Research in Black
Culture: 22, 27, 48, 61, 72, 104;
The Highlander Center and the Tennessee State Library
& Archives: 119; UPI/Bettmann: 10, 13, 15, 29, 41, 43,
51, 85, 86; UPI/Corbis-Bettmann: 6, 65, 95, 101.

Library of Congress Cataloging-in-Publication Data

Allen, Zita.
    Black women leaders of the civil rights movement / by Zita
    Allen.
        p.   cm. — (African-American experience)
    Includes bibliographical references and index.
    ISBN 0-531-11271-3
    1. Afro-American women civil rights workers—History—
20th century. 2. Afro-Americans—Civil rights—History—
20th century. 3. Civil rights movements—
United States—History—20th century. I. Title.
II. Series.
E185.61.A4415   1996
323.3'4'08996073—dc20                                    96-26134
                                                              CIP
                                                               AC

# TABLE OF CONTENTS

# 1

## INTRODUCTION

It was one of the defining moments of the civil rights movement: On August 28, 1963, the leaders of the movement stood on the steps of the Lincoln Memorial and looked out on the sea of humanity that had poured into the nation's capital for the historic March on Washington. They headed a vital cause that had swept across America, commanding the attention of the entire country. These leaders were credited with ushering in one of the most turbulent eras since the Civil War.

Shoulder to shoulder, heads bowed in prayer, were the anointed architects of the movement: A. Philip Randolph, Roy Wilkins, James Farmer, Whitney Young, and Dr. Martin Luther King, Jr., among others, all men.

On the steps of the Lincoln Memorial that bright, sundrenched August day, not a single woman delivered a major speech. Nor were any women asked to join the delegation summoned to the White House for a brief meeting with President John F. Kennedy following the era's crowning moment.[1]

Where were the women who played leadership roles in the civil rights movement? Some of them were in seats on the crowded steps of the Lincoln Memorial. Next to performers Lena Horne and Josephine Baker were Dorothy Height of the National Council of Negro Women and Gloria Richardson Dandridge, head of the Maryland-based Cambridge Movement.

Gloria Richardson Dandridge recalls, "I was one of the women being honored and when I got up there I was busy talking and networking. Bayard Rustin came after me and said, 'You know, they're all on the platform; come, let me take you up there.' He led me through the crowd, and when I got there Lena Horne and Josephine Baker were sitting in the first two places in the front line.

"I said, 'Well, where am I supposed to sit?'

"Somebody else said, 'You need to raise hell, they took your chair away.'

"I said, 'I'm not going to raise hell.' And I went all the way in the back so when the time came for them to announce that I was supposed to speak, they had to call me. I came up to the mike, and I wanted to tell the crowd to sit there until Congress passed the Civil Rights Act. I said, 'Hello' and before I knew it, somebody from the NAACP came up and took the mike away from me. To the best of my recollection, no other women spoke that day."[2]

Activist lawyer Dr. Pauli Murray remembers that day too: "It was bitterly humiliating for black women to see themselves accorded little more than token recognition in the historic March on Washington. Not a single woman was invited to make one of the major speeches or be part of the delegation of leaders who went to the White House. This omission was deliberate. Representations for recognition of women were made to the policy-making body sufficiently in advance of August 28 to have permitted the necessary adjustments in the program. What black women were told is revealing: that no representation was given to them because they would not be able to agree on a delegate."[3]

Dandridge and Murray had been chosen to represent the hundreds of women who had been both leaders and members of the movement's army of activists. There they were on the sidelines, relegated to the shadows until summoned like the movement's handmaidens, when in fact they had been its bricklayers.

Studies of the civil rights movement have traditionally focused on a few organizations—the Southern Christian Leadership Conference (SCLC), the Student Nonviolent Coordinating Committee (SNCC), the National Association for the Advancement of Colored People (NAACP), and the Congress of Racial Equality (CORE)—and the men who led them. In these accounts, men are at the center of the yearlong Montgomery Bus Boycott in the mid-1950s, the student sit-ins that swept the South in the early 1960s, and the massive voter registration drives. Usually, only one or two women are mentioned as having some influence in this historic period: Ella Baker, as executive secretary of SCLC; Fannie Lou Hamer, as grassroots organizer in the Deep South; and Rosa Parks, as an inspirational figure and catalyst.

Women were extremely influential members of SNCC, SCLC, and the Mississippi Freedom Democratic Party. According to Dorothy Height, "Black women are the backbone of every institution, but sometimes they are not recognized as even being there, even in the civil rights movement."4

## Montgomery Bus Boycott

Women were the spark that touched off a number of the era's most prominent protests, protests that historians often describe as led by black ministers. Leadership of the Montgomery bus boycott is often attributed to Martin Luther King, Jr., while the only woman credited with starting this action is Rosa Parks. She is generally described simply as a middle-aged seamstress who refused to relinquish her seat on a city bus to a white man. Actually, the force behind the Montgomery bus boycott was women—members of the Women's Political Council led by Jo Ann Robinson. The

*Constance Baker Motley (right) and Mrs. Martin Luther King, Jr.,
in 1965.*

boycott was not started by King or any of the city's other black ministers.

## Brown v. Board of Education

Thurgood Marshall and the lawyers of the NAACP Legal Defense and Education Fund were searching for cases to use as ammunition in the war against the South's segregated school system. Prince Edward County, Virginia, student leaders Ethel Belton and Dorothy Davis and the fiery sixteen-year-old leader Barbara Rose Johns were seeking justice. They asked their parents to contact the NAACP.[5] Eventually, the Prince Edward County case became one of five in the Supreme Court's 1954 *Brown v. Board of Education* decision.

Women fresh out of the nation's most prestigious law schools were among the legal architects of the NAACP strategy. Constance Baker Motley and Marian Wright Edelman were on Thurgood Marshall's team at the NAACP Legal Defense and Education Fund. As African-American women lawyers, they were following in the footsteps of such impressive activist attorneys as Sadie Tanner Mossell Alexander, the first black woman admitted to the bar in Pennsylvania in 1927.

In 1945, just out of Columbia Law School, Motley was the first female lawyer to join the NAACP Legal Defense and Education Fund. At the time, women lawyers, especially black women lawyers, were a rarity in most courthouses. When Marshall sent Motley to argue a case in Jackson, Mississippi, in 1949, the entire town turned out to see the "Nigra lawyers" from New York. Once, a Mississippi judge caused a stir when he addressed her as Mrs. Motley. This showed respect that was unique at a time when whites often addressed all blacks by their first names.[6]

Motley argued some of the country's most famous school desegregation cases, including Autherine Lucy's attempt to gain admission to the University of Alabama, James Meredith's 1962 bid to enter the University of Mississippi, and

Charlayne Hunter and Hamilton Holmes's 1961 case for admission to the University of Georgia.

She recalls accompanying Marshall to virtually every case he argued, including *Brown v. Board of Education.* "I participated in civil rights cases in federal courts in eleven states and the District of Columbia. Out of the ten cases I argued before the United States Supreme Court, I won nine. One particularly busy day in 1962, I argued four cases on appeal in the Fifth Circuit Court."[7] All this was at a time when women lawyers rarely went before the United States Supreme Court. When traveling, Motley was forced to stay in homes heavily guarded by men with machine guns and in "Negro" hotels in the "Negro" section of town.

When she left the fund in February 1965 to become the first woman president of the Borough of Manhattan and, a year later, the first African American and the second woman ever elected to the New York State Senate, Motley was one of the best-known civil rights lawyers in the country.

Yale Law School graduate Marian Wright Edelman was another one of a generation of black women lawyers who left their mark on civil rights cases. Working with the NAACP in Jackson, Mississippi, in the spring of 1964, she was the state's first black woman lawyer. "It's amazing what you can come to accept as part of your life, like starting up your car in the morning with the door open in case there's a bomb. Bombs were going off all the time that summer, but you learn how to deal with that fear, and with the fear of being shot at; you learn how to function in spite of it," she once said.[8]

## Little Rock Central High School

Daisy Bates led the charge when blacks in Little Rock, Arkansas, decided to implement the Supreme Court's school desegregation ruling. Bates was president of the local NAACP chapter and with her husband, L. C. Bates, served as crusading editor and publisher of the *Arkansas State Press,* a black weekly newspaper. Despite bomb threats, crosses

*The Little Rock Nine meet in a study group. (From left, seated on the floor) Thelma Mothershed, Elizabeth Eckford, and Melba Pattillo; (seated above) Jefferson Thomas, Ernest Green, Minniejean Brown, Carlotta Walls, Terrence Roberts, and Gloria Ray.*

burned in her front yard, and constant telephone harassment by white racists, she did not give up. According to Bates, "When we took on segregation in the Little Rock schools, I don't think we had any big idea that we were going to win it then. But they were gonna know they had had a fight!"[9]

Six of the youngsters putting their lives on the line in front of angry mobs were girls. One in particular—fourteen-year-old Elizabeth Eckford—became an international symbol of the youths' quiet dignity and courage when she faced a mob alone. The crowd was shouting epithets, spitting at her, and even threatening to lynch her as she clutched her schoolbooks and walked the gauntlet to Central High School.

## The Sit-ins

There was the legendary Fannie Lou Hamer, a sharecropper on a southern plantation in Ruleville, Mississippi, who risked everything to join the movement. Diane Nash was a campus beauty queen from one of the traditional black colleges, Fisk University in Nashville, Tennessee. Outraged at the South's Jim Crow segregation, this Chicago-born youngster was a student leader of the sit-in demonstrations at segregated lunch counters.

"I remember realizing that with what we were trying to do, we were coming up against governors of seven states, judges, politicians, businessmen, and I remember thinking, 'I'm only twenty-two years old. What do I know? What am I doing?' I felt vulnerable. So when we heard that other cities had demonstrations, it really helped, because there were more of us. And I think we started feeling the power of an idea whose time had come," Nash said.[10]

Nash emphasized that the movement, despite media attention to big-name leaders, "was really a people's movement. Young people should realize that it was people just like them, their age, that formulated goals and strategies and actually developed the movement," she recalled.

## The University of Georgia

Charlayne Hunter-Gault had been just another young girl vying successfully to become homecoming queen of Turner High. Hunter-Gault recalled walking down the red-carpeted gymnasium floor wearing a "floor-length white satin gown with off-the-shoulder bodice, rhinestones, pearls, lace

*Charlayne Hunter-Gault with a bodyguard on the University of Georgia campus*

and a long garland of hand-made white silk flowers and green leaves."[11] This is the stuff teenage years are made of. The next year she became the first black woman to enter the University of Georgia in its 176-year history. Charlayne Hunter could hear the shouts of rioting white students chanting "Two, four, six, eight, we don't want to integrate" outside her dormitory room.

A native of Birmingham, Alabama, Angela Davis was a fourteen-year-old gangly girl attending school in New York, and homesick for her family, when she joined her friends to picket the F. W. Woolworth store on Forty-second Street in a show of solidarity with southern blacks.

Later, with hundreds of other students from around the

country, Diane Nash helped found the Student Non-violent Coordinating Committee. Its youthful leadership infused the movement with astounding energy and enthusiasm as it led a blitz of sit-ins, freedom rides, and voter registration drives. Both Angela Davis and Charlayne Hunter became part of a force that changed the world.

Women leaders in quest of justice acted in the tradition of Sojourner Truth, Mary McLeod Bethune, Harriet Tubman, Ida B. Wells, and others. In 1897, the National Association of Colored Women (NACW) had over five thousand members devoted to women's advancement and justice and equality for all blacks. Mary McLeod Bethune went on to found the National Council of Negro Women (NCNW), to give black women a voice in national affairs. Subsequent leaders built on this premise. Dorothy Irene Height, the fourth president of NCNW, who was at the helm during the turbulent civil rights era, boasted that the NCNW represented four million women. When Height obtained tax exempt status for the NCNW, the organization's clout grew. It became known for its ability to implement major government-sponsored programs. As proof of this reputation, it received sizable grants from government and nongovernmental agencies. The NCNW, from 1965 to 1980, sponsored some forty projects related to youth and women's issues: day care centers, health care projects, immunization programs, and more. Recently, the organization has emphasized the strength and traditional values of the black family.

In male-dominated organizations, such as the NAACP and the National Urban League, women played more traditional, supportive roles. Often they were given the job of raising funds, boosting membership, or providing administrative support for the male leadership. In women's organizations, on the other hand, they were able to flex their muscles.

The civil rights era would see several women in these male-dominated organizations emerge as leaders in specific struggles. Modejeska Simpkins, a key force in the NAACP's South Carolina branch in the 1940s and 1950s, served as corresponding secretary, director of publicity, and state secretary. She played a pivotal role in the battle to equalize teachers' salaries in 1944 and in the lawsuits to dismantle the all-white primary, as well as in the school desegregation cases that later became known as *Brown v. Board of Education*. Simpkins' most valuable assets were her diligence and defiance, best characterized by her words "I cannot be bought and I will not be sold." Simpkins was from one of the state's wealthy black families and had a brother who was president of the black-owned and -operated Victory Savings Bank of Columbia, South Carolina.[12] Yet the national leadership of the older civil rights organizations was male. When the movement got off the ground, women emerged as leaders not in the NAACP or Urban League or other, more traditional, male-dominated organizations, but in the newer, less traditional groups like the Student Non-violent Coordinating Committee. Even in SNCC, problems eventually emerged when the debate over the role of women within the movement reached high decibel levels.

This "was a debate that destroyed the organization because it collapsed as a result of the intransigence of male leadership with respect to our feelings as women," according to Angela Davis, who joined SNCC in Los Angeles in the late 1960s. Davis said, "The women's liberation movement developed out of the civil rights movement. Younger women saw the contributions that women like Fannie Lou Hamer, Daisy Bates, Ella Baker, Septima Clark [made]... and the role they were playing vis-à-vis the male leadership.

"Women like Jo Ann Robinson did all this work for a number of years, and Rosa Parks was organizing to make it possible for the Montgomery bus boycott to take place, but when it did, it was Dr. King who received all the historical credit for it. Rosa Parks is not represented as a longtime civil rights organizer but as simply someone who got tired one day and didn't stand up."[13]

As a result of the discussion within SNCC about the role of women in that organization in the South, SNCC women created the Black Women's Commission, which eventually broke away from SNCC to become the Black Women's Alliance, and later evolved into the Third World Women's Alliance. Prompted by experiences in the civil rights movement, women would insist that the dialogue focus on the kind of triple jeopardy experienced by black women and women of color—racism, sexism, and economic exploitation. Essentially, this dialogue was a continuation of one begun years earlier.

While there were no women standing with the anointed leaders on the steps of the Lincoln Memorial that sparkling sunny day in August 1963, there were women, young and old, in the forefront, leading the protests of the decade that led to that moment and beyond. This is the story of some of them.

# 2

# THE PAST AS PROLOGUE: LAYING THE GROUNDWORK FOR THE CIVIL RIGHTS MOVEMENT

In the first half of this century the foundation for the civil rights period was laid. At the heart of this activity from 1900 to 1950 was the drive by hundreds of black women to lift the race out of poverty and social and political bondage — the black women's club movement. A successful network of self-help organizations, the club movement was a response to issues created by the large numbers of blacks migrating from the South to the northern urban areas.

The heat generated by the debate over lynching sparked the formation of the National Association of Colored Women (NACW) headed by Mary Church Terrell.

## NATIONAL ASSOCIATION OF COLORED WOMEN

Three groups were instrumental in forming the nationwide organization: the National League of Colored Women in Washington, D.C., headed by Mary Church Terrell; the National Federation of Afro-American Women, headed by Margaret Murray Washington; and the Women's Era Club in Boston, headed by Josephine St. Pierre Ruffin, the first black female publisher of a monthly magazine, *Women's Era*.

*Antilynching protest in Washington, D.C., in 1934*

The catalyst for the NACW's formation was a slander-ous letter from a southern journalist lambasting Ida B. Wells's antilynching campaign and attacking all black women as having no sense of virtue and of being without character. Ruffin published the letter in her magazine ac-companied by a call for a national black women's confer-ence in Boston.

When leaders formalized the group's structure at an 1897 meeting in Nashville, Tennessee, the NACW was already a national organization representing over five thousand women. By 1899, at its first biennial conference in Chicago, an ideological rift developed that would resurface in the black community in subsequent decades. The battle between conciliatory integrationist forces and more aggressive separatist ones would rear its head during the civil rights struggles of the 1960s. For the next four decades, the NACW was a major vehicle through which black women attempted reform. It devoted itself to their protection and advancement, as well as to the fight for justice and equality for all blacks.

In the years before World War I the NACW grew rapidly. In 1901, there was one regional and six state federations. By 1916, there were three hundred new clubs. Motivated by a philosophy of service that stressed the responsibility of the "haves" to help the "have nots," the club women created and supported countless institutions. They founded homes for the aged, such as the Gabriella Smith Home for Aged and Infirm Colored People in Chicago, Elizabeth Carter's Home for the Aged in New Bedford, and the Phyllis Wheatley Home for Aged Colored Women in Detroit. They supported hospital wards for African Americans and even entire black hospitals. They also founded and supported a tuberculosis camp, orphanages, kindergartens, and settlement houses for young women. New York's White Rose Home, for young working girls, was a model for similar institutions.

While the common desire to uplift the race held the NACW together, how that should best be done and who should spearhead the process were two key questions. The same questions would plague other groups during the 1960s' civil rights movement. At the center of the group's ideological conflict were the philosophies of two titans battling for the hearts and minds of the community-at-large during those times—Booker T. Washington and W. E. B. Du Bois.

Booker T. Washington's beliefs in vocational education for blacks and in compromise in social and political struggles made him acceptable to several presidential administrations, and elevated him from head of Tuskegee Institute to the position of main broker of patronage for blacks. Harvard-educated W. E. B. Du Bois, founder of the Niagara Movement and later one of the founders of the NAACP, believed, however, that blacks should take a more aggressive stance in the pursuit of justice. He held that blacks should strengthen their own institutions rather than fight to integrate white ones and that a well-educated cadre of black leaders or talented tenth, must come forth. According to Du Bois, racial segregation and racial discrimination were two different issues, and integration for its own sake was meaningless.

Militant and assertive, Ida B. Wells had much in common with Du Bois, while Mary Church Terrell's more conciliatory tone betrayed close ties to Booker T. Washington's accommodationist philosophy.

## National Association for the Advancement of Colored People

Even as women nurtured their own organizations, they continued to play the traditional supportive roles in the development of male-dominated institutions such as the National Association for the Advancement of Colored People (NAACP), its predecessor, the Niagara Movement, and the National Urban League.

The NAACP was founded in 1909 after a bloody race riot in 1908 in Springfield, Illinois. This riot prompted a small group of white reformers to issue a call through Oswald Garrison Villard of the *New York Evening Post*. The

*Charlotte Hawkins Brown*

call was for all the believers in democracy to join in a national conference for the discussion of present evils, the voicing of protests and the renewal of the struggle for civil and political liberty. A thousand invitations beckoned interested reformers, community leaders, and educators to the first conference of the National Negro Committee in New York, May 31 and June 1, 1909. Both Ida B. Wells and Mary Church Terrell attended. They were appointed to the committee responsible for designing a permanent organization together with a third black woman, Maria Baldwin. Black women would play a prominent role in the development of the leadership network, which would help spread the philosophy, raise money, and increase membership in the NAACP, from the very beginning. While a black woman was deftly passed over when the time came for the organization to select its first black national field organizer (James Weldon Johnson took that post), black women had opened the way for black male leadership in the organization.

According to Mary White Ovington, a white woman who was one of the NAACP's founding leaders, "Our Advancement Association would be a mere National Negro Committee but for the organized work of the women in the branches." Ovington acknowledged the tremendously important role black women played in grassroots organizing to build the NAACP's membership. Many of these women utilized the network developed through their flourishing club movement.

Black women's hard work as field workers and branch participants in male-dominated organizations did not automatically translate to high-level positions in the national administration. But it helped in the ascendancy of black male leadership. James Weldon Johnson's appointment as national organizer in 1916, and national secretary in 1920, was due to the growing black membership sparked by the successful grassroots organizing of women. Not until Myrlie Evers was elected executive director in 1994 did a woman assume total leadership of the organization.

# National Urban League

The National Urban League sprang up in 1911 from the merger of a number of organizations that provided social services. Three of the primary groups were the National League for the Protection of Colored Women, the Committee for Improving Industrial Conditions in New York, and the Committee on Urban Conditions among Negroes. The League relied heavily on the networks developed by black women in the club movement, settlement houses, and other community organizations.

Founded in 1908, the Neighborhood Union in Atlanta, under the direction of founding president Lugenia Burns Hope, provided a model of organization. From city to city, as black migrants reached town, helpful club women met them at train and bus stations and wherever new arrivals gathered, and helped them locate housing, jobs, and schools.

In addition to providing such bread-and-butter assistance, the Urban League's journal, *Opportunity*, opened its pages to literary and visual artists who were women. In 1925, the first year of the famous *Opportunity* contest, seven of its playwright awards went to works authored by women, including Zora Neale Hurston.

As the league developed, it proved to be quite a different organization from the NAACP. Again, women were chiefly relegated to positions of fund-raisers and membership boosters, and were not major cogs in the organization's administrative wheels.

The league did not blossom quite as profusely as the NAACP. By the end of 1919, while the NAACP had 310 branches with 88,292 members, the league had only 27 affiliates by 1918 and 34 by 1930. The NAACP's larger membership lessened its financial dependence on a small group of wealthy whites. Black women in the NAACP were its major fund-raisers, while in the Urban League, over 40 percent of its budget in those early days came from three wealthy white patrons. Although during its early years, the

NAACP's membership was dominated by white reformers, gradually, with the help of black women fund-raisers, the black funding allowed the emergence of black leadership, albeit male, and a somewhat more aggressive political justice agenda.

## National Council of Negro Women

Mary McLeod Bethune founded the National Council of Negro Women (NCNW) on December 5, 1935. Bethune was president of the Florida Federation of Colored Women's Clubs (1917 to 1924), founder and president of the Southeastern Association of Colored Women (1920 to 1925), and eighth president of the National Association of Colored Women. Bethune wanted to create one organization that was an umbrella for hundreds of others. This led to the creation of the NCNW. Bethune was also concerned that black women were putting their energy into fund-raising for male-dominated organizations and male-defined causes and not enough into issues crucial to black women.

Bethune's initiative was truly visionary. She skillfully used her position as head of the NCNW to make her friendship with the first lady, Eleanor Roosevelt, count for something. President Franklin D. Roosevelt appointed blacks to his administration in unprecedented numbers. He named Bethune director of the Negro Division of the National Youth Administration. Together with her post as NCNW head, Bethune had all the leverage she needed, unprecedented power for an African-American woman.

With Bethune at the helm, the NCNW focused on public affairs, employment, citizenship, family life, religion, consumer education, and more. In monitoring employment discrimination in plants engaged in war work, the NCNW

*Mary McLeod Bethune*

brought pressure that triggered the creation of the Fair Employment Practice Commission. Bethune fought for the admission of black women into the women's divisions of the navy, army, and air force. As a result, black women were admitted to the Women's Army Corps.

Under Bethune, the NCNW formed coalitions with a host of other organizations, including the NAACP, the National Urban League, the League of Women Voters, the National Council of Church Women, the National Council of Jewish Women, and the National Council of Catholic Women, as they worked together on programs targeting the elimination of racism and sexism.

As a strong supporter of international struggles for peace, Bethune was one of two NAACP consultants who attended the founding meeting of the United Nations in San Francisco, thus also representing the NCNW at the gathering. When she left office in 1949, the NCNW was the major black women's organization in the civil rights arena.

The association continued to grow under Bethune's hand-picked successor, Dorothy Boulding Ferebee (1949 to 1953), and under Vivian Carter Mason (1953 to 1957). Under Mason, the NCNW worked closely with the NAACP to find ways to implement the 1954 Supreme Court ruling on segregated schools by revving up the organization's vast network. In 1956, the council's twenty-first annual convention was an interracial conference of women committed to surmounting the barriers to human and civil rights.

Dorothy Irene Height (1957 to present) took over as fourth president of the National Council of Negro Women on the eve of the heightened civil rights struggle in the 1960s. Steering it through a difficult transition, Height was at the helm during a time of phenomenal growth.

In the late 1930s, Bethune often boasted that the NCNW represented some fifty thousand women. Under Height, the number grew to four million women.

*In 1946 the National Association of Colored Women picketed the White House to protest lynching.*

# 3

## FOREMOTHERS OF THE REVOLUTION — 1939-1946

In 1940, two leaders of the Southern Negro Youth Congress (SNYC), Ed Strong and James Jackson, drove Esther Cooper, a twenty-one-year-old graduate of Oberlin College, to the edge of a backwater plantation town in Alabama. Cooper stepped out of the car onto a dirt road and prepared to make a lonely walk into town. The Southern Negro Youth Congress had gotten word that the town's white sheriff had ordered every black man, woman, and child to stay indoors until he lifted his arbitrarily imposed curfew, or else they'd be shot. SNYC's mission was to find out if the rumor was true, and if so, develop a strategy that would force the sheriff to rescind his order and, in Cooper's words, "open up the town." Cooper had bravely volunteered to enter the town, although she knew absolutely no one and would have to chance it that perfect strangers would take her in, tell her what was happening and, if anyone asked, say that she was a visiting relative.[1]

Cooper stood alone beneath a scorching southern sun, attired in a little cotton dress and socks, poised to investigate yet another instance of arbitrary racial terror. At this time, elected officials took no notice of such injustices and federal agencies generally turned a deaf ear to any calls for help. The young woman was prepared to use whatever tools were at her disposal to change the situation.

Esther Cooper came out of that town before sundown with enough material to pass along to the few national newspapers that took an interest in such stories. She had also collected information for Ed Strong and James Jackson to use to mount a campaign against such senseless violence against blacks.

She had met Jackson at Fisk in 1939, when he was a researcher and writer for sociologist Gunnar Myrdal, who would later publish the highly acclaimed study *The Negro in America: An American Dilemma*. After being awarded a bachelor of arts degree from Oberlin, she received a master's degree in history and sociology from Fisk University in Nashville, Tennessee, in 1938.

Her plans were to continue postgraduate work at the University of Chicago. Then, a telegram came from Strong and Jackson, offering her a summer job at twenty-five dollars a week with SNYC's voter registration campaign based in Birmingham, Alabama. In those days, Birmingham's black business area was just a two-block stretch of small mom-and-pop stores and restaurants. There was Bob's Savoy Restaurant, one "colored" movie theater, and Nancy's Cafe, where Jackson and Strong took her to lunch when she arrived to begin work.

Esther recalls, "We sat down to eat, and the first thing Ed and Jack (Jackson) asked me was, how much money did I have? They were supposed to be paying me! They said they had to get the typewriter out of hock, and they had some other bills. So I took my last three hundred dollars and gave it to them. That was my introduction to SNYC!" Founded in Richmond, Virginia, on February 17, 1937, the Southern Negro Youth Congress had grown out of the National Negro Congress, a diverse coalition of organizations from the NAACP to the Communist party, devoted to fighting for social, political, and economic justice for African Americans. The several hundred young people attending the 1936 National Negro Congress had insisted on elbow room to express themselves. As result, SNYC was founded. When the new group's first conference was held, 534 delegates from throughout the South attended. Many were student activists, sharecroppers, and hardworking men and women from America's fledgling labor unions. Affiliated groups included such powerhouses as the NAACP, the National Council of Negro Women, the United Mine Workers of America, the United Steel Workers, and other labor unions.

When the Southern Negro Youth Congress was founded, the African-American struggle for civil rights had a two-pronged focus. On one hand there was a massive campaign to destroy one of the most vicious forms of extralegal terror against blacks—lynching. When a black man was suspected of a crime—some imagined or real infraction of the unspoken rules of this divided society—a mob would hang him before he could have a trial.

On the other hand, there was a campaign to destroy the tangled web of legislation that had developed after the Civil War. These laws, in often rococo detail, were southern white society's feverish attempt to keep its boot on the back of the formerly enslaved blacks. At the heart of this system was the refusal to allow close to half of the population in the South to exercise a fundamental right of American citizens—the right to vote.

The Southern Negro Youth Congress, which thrived from 1937 to 1949, was a branch of the same tree that produced those civil rights organizations whose names are synonymous with the 1960s—the Southern Christian Leadership Conference, the Student Non-violent Coordinating Committee, the Congress of Racial Equality, and others. SNYC focused on mobilizing the young people in the fight for political and economic equality.

As with many civil rights organizations, black women

made a tremendous contribution to the Southern Negro Youth Congress. But, for years historians have ignored the women who played roles in the founding and development of these groups, serving as organizers, office staff, publication editors, and just general guiding lights. In some cases, women were not highly visible because they were deliberately pushed into the background. This was not the case with the Southern Negro Youth Congress, Cooper says. Women were encouraged to take the lead.

"When I first went to work with SNYC, males did dominate the scene. Ed Strong and James Jackson, two of the founders, were the dominant forces in the organization. When I became the executive secretary of the group, it was the first time a woman was elevated to a major position." Cooper was the first woman to head a major civil rights organization.

According to Cooper, this change took place with the support of SNYC's male leadership. "I was a little timid when I first came to work with SNYC," Cooper recalls. "I had never worked in the Deep South and I felt like an interloper. At first, I volunteered to pass out fliers, or go into some town where we had to investigate reports of brutality toward blacks, but they insisted that I become a spokesperson."

Frequently, the women of SNYC helped the organization form coalitions by reaching out to the women's auxiliary of other community organizations, trade unions, and church groups. Cooper says meeting with the wives of the coal miners and steel workers was very helpful. "At first, the wives were suspicious of these young women who were doing organizing work with their husbands, but we included them in activities. Eventually, we started holding discussion groups with them in our homes. We started out by examining the role of women in our society, then narrowed it down to the role of women in the SNYC. The group grew because we wanted to get to know the women better."

Women played a major role in all of the group's campaigns: the antipoll tax movement, led by Augusta Strong, massive voter registration campaigns, a series of politically-inspired cultural events, and the running of SNYC's leadership-training schools.

Cooper says the issues most pressing for SNYC's women were in many ways the same issues of importance to its men—the right to vote, jobs, dignity in the workplace, better schools, libraries, and public accommodations. Cooper recalls one campaign to integrate a public park in the middle of Birmingham, Alabama. The park sat directly across the street from the Sixteenth Street Baptist Church. (In 1963, during the civil rights struggle, a bomb exploded in this same church and killed four young black children.) Wooden benches lined the paths of the tiny vest-pocket park in the heart of the black neighborhood. "This park was deeded to the city of Birmingham by some white man in his will, with a stipulation that no black person had the right to sit down on a bench there in the middle of the black community. Every black person walked through the park on their way to jobs, or shopping, or to visit friends," Cooper said.

In 1941, she led the struggle so that blacks who were tired and walking home from work could stop and sit down in that park and rest for a moment. Cooper and others collected thousands of signatures on petitions denouncing the segregation of this little park. She shocked the all-white male Birmingham City Council when she appeared before them to present the petitions.

"They turned all kinds of colors," she recalls. "When I came walking down the long aisle leading to the speaker's desk with this stack of petitions, my very presence shocked them. Mayor Cooper Green and the infamous Sheriff Eugene "Bull" Connor were there. They said 'Alright, what do you have to say, girl?'

"I said, 'My name is Esther Cooper Jackson and I'm a mother, not a girl.' They just sat there. They didn't know what to think. They were so taken aback that, ordinarily, they would have told me to get out of the chambers, but they were too stunned to respond. Finally, I argued the case on the basis that this park was in the black community.

"They accepted my petitions, but it took another year of pressure from the churches and the trade unions, including the United Mine Workers, before blacks could sit in that little park. Even then, it took some time before blacks felt at ease enough to sit on the benches. Many felt uncomfortable. They were afraid they'd be dragged away by the police, or lynched for just daring to sit on a park bench. We used to go in and sit to give people the inspiration to try it. Now, what's so ironic about it is that today there is a statue of Martin Luther King, Jr., in that park" (and a civil rights museum down the street).

On the heels of the park incident came another in which Esther Cooper locked horns with Birmingham's political establishment. In 1942, SNYC scheduled a rally under the banner "For Victory over Hitler and Jim Crow at Home." The rally was to bolster African-American support for World War II, and Vice President Henry Wallace had accepted an invitation to speak.

James Jackson had to meet with the mayor to get permission to use the city's stadium for a gathering that was expected to draw twenty thousand people. Also in attendance were Sheriff Bull Connor and the director of Parks and Playgrounds. According to Jackson, "Mayor Green and the others questioned the need to have U.S. Vice President Henry Wallace at the meeting. Mayor Green said, 'Well, I don't see what you need Wallace down here for. You know, we had these Eleanor clubs when Eleanor Roosevelt came down and she came arm in arm with that black woman, Mary McLeod Bethune. Now, Bull jumped up and down in the air and it took all I could do to keep explaining to him that this was the President's wife. We agreed to put a rope down the aisle because this Eleanor woman wanted to have the blacks and the whites all mixed up in the city auditorium. Now, we couldn't have that. Look a here, why don't you have those gospel singing clubs and one or two local speakers?'

"Sheriff Bull Connor added, 'One person you can't have there is this Esther Cooper woman. She's going to get a lot of Negroes killed in this town.'"

James Jackson recalls turning his chair around so that he was looking squarely in the mayor's face. Then he told Green that he planned to guarantee the health and safety of the Cooper woman because she happened to be his wife.

Esther Cooper joined the ranks of countless unsung heroines of the civil rights movement. Years later, when she and James Jackson continued to organize in the Deep South, she would go toe to toe with the city council in Birmingham, Alabama. She endured the sneers of Sheriff Bull Connor, who would go on to play a larger role in the unfolding drama.

A brochure announcing the sixth All-Southern Negro Youth Conference in Atlanta, Georgia, November 30 to December 3, 1944, bragged that the SNYC was "dedicated to the task of strengthening American democracy through the improvement of the conditions and opportunities of Negro youth."

Its program of action was described in the *Souvenir Journal* of the Columbia, South Carolina, convention of October 18 to 20, 1946:

> (1) to make ourselves a full-fledged voting generation;
> (2) to see that the poll-tax and all barriers to the vote are removed;
> (3) to realize the enactment of an F.E.P.C. law guaranteeing the right to work at all jobs;
> (4) to fight for federal anti-lynching legislation and genuine civil liberties;

(5) to insist on adequate and equal housing, health and educational facilities;

(6) to put an end to "white supremacy" customs and practices which violate our human dignity and rights.

Included in its impressive roster of leaders were Dr. W. E. B. Du Bois, a founder of the NAACP, and Dr. Charlotte Hawkins Brown, a member of the National Council of Negro Women. James Jackson was the chief researcher in the South. The list of rank-and-file members was equally impressive. Augusta Jackson Strong was the editor of *Cavalcade—The March of Southern Negro Youth*. Sallie Bell Davis, a young university student, had become a leader of the civil rights struggle in her hometown of Birmingham, Alabama. Years later, during the 1960s, her daughter, Angela Davis, would rise to international prominence. Thelma Dale Perkins, from Washington, D.C., had been an activist at Howard University and knew Ed Strong and James Jackson when they were in graduate school there. Many early civil rights activists came out of Howard University.

The Southern Negro Youth Congress held a unique place in the years before the civil rights movement exploded on the scene. Dorothy Burnham, SNYC's educational director, presided over research, publications, and publicity. She later married Louis E. Burnham, another founder of the organization. Louis Burnham would become known throughout the South as a noted civil rights lawyer. He worked on the case of Emmett Till, a fourteen-year-old who was brutally beaten and murdered in Greenwood, Mississippi, for allegedly whistling at a white woman.

In 1960, an idea for a magazine was suggested by Louis Burnham, who had been the editor of Paul Robeson's newspaper, *Freedom*. Burnham talked to his friends Esther and James Jackson and Dr. Du Bois and his wife, Shirley Graham, about starting a quarterly publication. When Esther was asked to help get it started, she agreed to "give it a couple of years." Unfortunately, Burnham died before it got off the ground. So Shirley Graham, Dr. Du Bois, the Jacksons, and a number of writers and artists took over the magazine. The first issue of *Freedomways* came out in the spring of 1961. Instead of giving it a few years, Esther edited it for the next twenty-five, working with an illustrious roster of contributing writers, activists, and artists, including James Baldwin, Alice Walker, and Elizabeth Catlett.

# 4

## INTEGRATING THE SCHOOLS
## 1954–1959

P inpointing the exact moment the civil rights movement began is not easy. Since first setting foot on
American soil, African Americans have struggled for
the freedom to exercise the same rights as all other citizens.
Did the civil rights movement begin May 17, 1954, when
Chief Justice Earl Warren handed down the Supreme Court
decision that struck a blow at the heart of Jim Crow by de-
claring segregated schools unconstitutional? Did it start on
December 1, 1955, when Rosa Parks refused to get up from
her seat on a Montgomery, Alabama, city bus so that a
white man could sit? Or was it triggered on February 1,
1960, in Greensboro, North Carolina, when four black college students defied custom and sat down at a dime-store
lunch counter and asked to be served?

Was the disgust with Jim Crow segregation and the tangled web of terror and brutality that sustained it heightened
by the gruesome sight of the mutilated body of little fourteen-year-old Emmett Till? Thousands, after all, had filed
past the boy's open coffin in a Chicago funeral parlor after
his grief-stricken mother brought his body home.

For many, the civil rights era began with the Supreme
Court's 1954 *Brown v. Board of Education* decision and

ended in 1965, the year President Lyndon Baines Johnson declared "We shall overcome" as he proposed the Voting Rights Act to a joint session of Congress, March 15, 1965.

Chief Justice Earl Warren leaned forward from his judicial bench in the ornate chambers of the United States Supreme Court and announced a unanimous ruling in the case of *Oliver Brown et al. v. Board of Education of Topeka, Kansas*. Warren's decision took the nation by surprise, caught the press off guard, and triggered a chain of events that sent the country into a whirlwind of change.

*Brown v. Board of Education* was one of five cases brought to the Supreme Court.[1] This particular case centered on a seven-year-old girl named Linda Brown. Her father, Oliver Brown, was fed up with his child having to cross railroad tracks in a switching yard and wait for a rickety bus to take her miles away to a black school when a white school was three blocks from her house.[2]

The Supreme Court's decision in this packet of cases knocked down one of the principal pillars of America's form of apartheid. While it may be true that the civil rights movement did not start on May 17, 1954, *Brown* opened the door to a decade of unprecedented changes.

*Brown* was a major victory for a strategy developed two decades earlier under the guidance of Charles Houston, head of Howard University's School of Law. The NAACP's lawyers had set out to destroy the legal foundation of the South's racist society by chipping away at the Supreme Court's 1895 *Plessy v. Ferguson* case. This decision had established the legality of everything from separate water fountains and bathrooms to separate elementary schools and law schools. Thurgood Marshall, later the first black appointed to the Supreme Court, was one of many illustrious members of the NAACP's legal team, which had started out as all male. By the time Chief Justice Earl Warren leaned forward and pronounced that "in the field of public education the doctrine of 'separate but equal' has no place," there was one female lawyer on the NAACP Legal Defense Fund's team—Constance Baker Motley. Motley had joined

Constance Baker Motley (left), James Meredith (center), and
Jack Greenberg (right). Motley and Greenberg were NAACP
lawyers supporting James Meredith, who was applying to the
University of Mississippi.

the NAACP Legal Defense and Education Fund team as a law clerk before graduating from Columbia Law School in 1946. Other women later added to the NAACP team were Yale Law School graduates Eleanor Holmes Norton, whose civil rights career began in the Student Non-violent Coordinating Committee in the 1960s, and Marian Wright Edelman, the future head of the Children's Defense Fund.

Other women also played major roles in the drama surrounding the *Brown* case. Fourteen-year-old Dorothy Davis, the daughter of a Prince Edward County, Virginia, farmer, was featured in this historic packet of cases. Davis was one of the 117 students who had participated in a strike at Moton High School in April 1951 that led to the filing of the case.

Fiery sixteen-year-old Barbara Rose Johns headed the protest against unequal educational facilities in Prince Edward County. For some time, blacks in the county had complained that the school was too small and the facilities too limited—there was no cafeteria or gym. After seeing their parents' pleas fall repeatedly on deaf ears, Johns engineered a strike of the school's 450 students. She also secured the support of the parents, as well as assistance from the NAACP, which led to the filing of the *Davis v. County School Board of Prince Edward County* case. Later, Johns moved to Montgomery, Alabama, to live with her uncle, who was fighting the poor treatment of blacks on the Montgomery city buses.

## Little Rock Central High School

Women also played a part in the implementation of the *Brown* decision. On September 4, 1957, petite fifteen-year-old Elizabeth Eckford stepped off a city bus not far from Little Rock, Arkansas, Central High School and on to center stage in one of the most riveting images of the civil rights era.[3] She strode past a throng of jeering whites and armed soldiers. Wearing her neatly pressed white dress with a black-and-white checked border, and clutching a notebook,

*Elizabeth Eckford surrounded by members of the press.*

she walked with the quiet dignity that belied the fear in her eyes, hidden behind sunglasses. Elizabeth Eckford thought, "Maybe I'll be safe if I walk down the block to the front entrance behind the guards."

At the corner when she tried to pass, one armed soldier from the Arkansas National Guard blocked her way and pointed across the street. "I pointed in the same direction and asked whether he meant for me to cross the street and walk down. He nodded 'yes.' I walked across the street, conscious of the crowd that stood there, but they moved away from me.

"For a moment all I could hear was the shuffling of their feet. Then someone shouted, 'Here she comes, get ready!' I moved away from the crowd on the sidewalk and into the street. If the mob came at me, I could then cross back over so the guards could protect me.

"The crowd moved in closer and then began to follow me, calling me names. I still wasn't afraid. Just a little bit nervous. Then my knees started to shake all of a sudden and I wondered whether I could make it to the center entrance a block away. It was the longest block I ever walked in my life.

"When I got in front of the school, I went up to a guard again. But this time he just looked straight ahead and didn't move to let me pass him. I didn't know what to do. Then I looked and saw the path leading to the front entrance a little further ahead. So I walked until I was right in front of the path to the front door....

"The crowd was quiet. I guess they were waiting to see what was going to happen. When I was able to steady my knees, I walked up to the guard who had let the white students in. He too didn't move. When I tried to squeeze past him, he raised his bayonet and then the other guards moved in and they raised their bayonets.

"They glared at me with a mean look and I was very frightened and didn't know what to do. I turned around and the crowd came toward me.

"They moved closer and closer. Somebody started yelling, 'Lynch her! Lynch her!'

"I tried to see a friendly face somewhere in the mob— someone who maybe would help. I looked into the face of an old woman and it seemed a kind face, but when I looked at her again, she spat at me.

"They came closer, shouting, 'No nigger bitch is going to get in our school. Get out of here!'

"I turned back to the guards but their faces told me I wouldn't get any help from them. Then I looked down the block and saw a bench at the bus stop. I thought, 'If I can only get there I will be safe.' I don't know why the bench seemed a safe place to me, but I started walking toward it. I tried to close my mind to what they were shouting, and kept saying to myself, 'If I can only make it to the bench I will be safe.'

"When I finally got there, I don't think I could have gone another step. I sat down and the mob crowded up and began shouting all over again. Someone hollered, 'Drag her over to this tree! Let's take care of that nigger.'"

Just then, Benjamin Fine, a writer for *The New York Times*, put his arm around this frightened young girl whose courage and grace in the face of unbridled hatred would captivate the world. He patted her shoulder, raised her chin and said, "Don't let them see you cry."

Soon after that a white woman, Grace Lorch, whose husband taught at a local black college, took the girl's life and her own into her hands and lead Elizabeth away from the mob and toward a bus.

Eckford recalls, "She tried to talk to me but I don't think I answered. I can't remember much about the bus ride, but the next thing I remember I was standing in front of the School for the Blind, where Mother works."

Elizabeth Eckford was one of nine youngsters—three boys and six girls—who had been selected to integrate the school of twelve thousand white students in September 1957. They were shepherded through the process by Daisy Bates, president of the Arkansas NAACP, and her husband, L. C. Bates. Bates was the founder and publisher of the *Arkansas State Press*, a black weekly newspaper noted for its crusading spirit and campaigns against police brutality and other forms of injustice affecting Arkansas's black community.

Little Rock had been considered "a liberal southern city" as recently as 1954, with its integrated library, parks, and public buses. Arkansas was one of a handful of southern

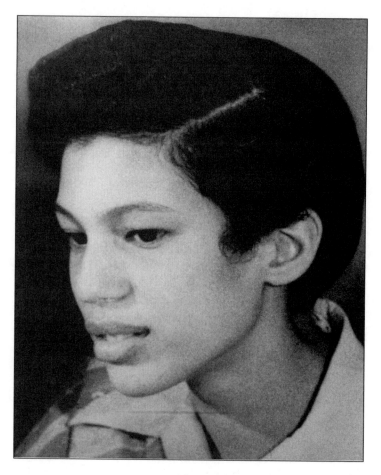

*Carlotta Walls*

states that had begun to implement the Supreme Court's *Brown* decision by desegregating their public schools. In 1954, Little Rock's school board had drawn up a gradual-phase plan that would limit integration to just one school and delay it until 1957. Yet, when the time came for the plan to be implemented, all hell broke loose.

The Little Rock Nine—Jefferson Thomas, Carlotta Walls, Gloria Ray, Elizabeth Eckford, Thelma Mothershed, Melba Pattilo, Terrence Roberts, Minniejean Brown, and Ernest Green—were poised to enter Central High School, the only school chosen by the Little Rock school board to be desegregated after it adopted the gradual phase program. A storm of vocal opposition to any form of desegregation was being mounted by the segregationist Capitol Citizens' Council. Eventually it stirred Arkansas Governor Orval Faubus to become part of what Daisy Bates described as the first serious confrontation between federal authorities and southern resistance to school desegregation.

"There was no thought on my part, on any of our parts, that our going to Central High would trigger this terrible catastrophe," Melba Pattilo Beals said later.[4] (After going on to graduate from Central High, Beals attended San Francisco State University and received a master's degree in journalism from Columbia University.)

"On the first day, the kinds of things that I endured were parents kicking, parents hitting, parents throwing things. You would get tripped; people would just walk up and hit you in the face. And, you couldn't hit back. We had been instructed that any attempts to hit back, to respond, to call a name would mean the end of the case," Beals recalls.

In the courtroom the NAACP lawyers battled the Little Rock school system's failure to comply with the Supreme Court's ruling to desegregate "with all deliberate speed."

Daisy Bates served as a rock of Gibraltar for children caught in the eye of a hurricane. Bates herself was threatened with retribution, as she recounts in her book, *The Long Shadow of Little Rock*. One night a rock was thrown through the large picture window of her home, with a note warning, "Brick this time, dynamite the next time." Phone calls late at night were often bomb threats; advertisers yanked their ads from the *Arkansas State Press*. Once the police followed a car driving slowly past her home with its lights off and found it carried dynamite and firearms. As head of the

*Daisy Bates (left)*

state's NAACP chapter, Bates was harassed by officials wanting to obtain copies of the group's membership lists. In those days, when membership in the NAACP could mean certain loss of a job, these lists were kept highly confidential.

"The phone rang constantly with threats. They broke the windows with rocks. They burned crosses in the yard all the time. Huge ones. And they set fire to the house. One night a man was going to throw a Molotov cocktail. I shot over his head with my .38 and he ducked and dropped it. Anther night the police caught some people with guns and ammunition enough to blow the whole town away. Dynamite everything! I was asked to stay with friends someplace else. I said, 'Why should I? This is my home. I live here. I'm gonna stay here.'" [5]

Little Rock became the first battlefield of the new civil rights movement. A collision course was set when Governor Orval Faubus announced on television the day before the schools were to open that he was surrounding the school with the National Guardsmen. Elizabeth Eckford encountered the guards that morning, September 4, and they remained while the school board asked the federal court to suspend the desegregation plan. The court refused, but Faubus did not budge, even after meeting with President Dwight Eisenhower, who urged him to comply with the district court's order. Eisenhower failed to put muscle behind his request until a full-scale riot broke out on September 23, when the students had finally entered the school—by way of a side entrance and under heavy guard.

"I'd only been in the school a couple of hours, and by this time it was apparent that the mob was overrunning the school. Policemen were throwing down their badges and the mob was getting past the wooden sawhorses because the police would no longer fight their own neighbors in order to protect us," Beals recalls. The children were called into the principal's office, where panicked adults and nine frightened black students tried to figure out what to do.

"Someone made the suggestion that if they allowed the mob to hang one kid, then they could get the rest out while they were hanging the one kid. And a gentleman whom I believed to be the police chief, said, 'How are you going to choose? You're going to let them draw straws?' He said, 'I'll get them out.' And we were taken to the basement of this place and put into two cars, grayish-blue Fords. The drivers were told, 'Once you start driving, do not stop.' They told us to put our heads down. So the guy revved up the engine and came out of the bowels of this building and as he came up, I could just see hands reaching across the car. I could hear the yelling. I could see guns. The driver didn't hit anybody, but

*Melba Pattillo Beals of the Little Rock Nine in 1977.*

he certainly was forceful and aggressive in the way he exited this driveway because people tried to stop him. He dropped me off at home, and I said, 'Thank you for the ride.' I should have said, 'Thank you for my life.'" Melba Pattillo Beals recalled this incident years later for interviewers of the *Eyes on the Prize* documentary on the civil rights era.

*The Little Rock Nine leaving Central High School under the protection of the federalized Arkansas National Guard.*

The riot forced President Eisenhower to take action. That evening he sent more than one thousand members of the 101st Airborne Division to Little Rock's Air Force Base. The Arkansas National Guard was also mobilized, and this time ordered to defend the black students. The president went on nationwide television to explain these actions.

The next morning, the Little Rock Nine met at Daisy Bates's house, as they had every morning, to be taken to school. This time they were escorted by a convoy of federal troops. One jeep was in front and one behind with machine gun mounts and soldiers armed with rifles. They went up the school steps guarded by 350 paratroopers, who lined two blocks of Park Avenue in front of the school, while helicopters hovered overhead. The commanding officer ordered the crowd to disperse. Inside the school, each student was assigned a military bodyguard, and at the end of the day they were escorted back to the Bates home.

Later, on September 31, the troops withdrew to a military base, leaving behind the federalized Arkansas National Guard to ensure order. Of course, incidents still occurred inside the school throughout the year. At one point, when Minniejean Brown had enough of being taunted in the lunch line, she picked up a bowl of chili and dumped it on the head of a white kid who had been harassing her. She was suspended. Whites in the school circulated cards reading "One down...eight to go." But on May 29, graduation day, the first of the Little Rock Nine graduated—Ernest Green. That summer, Governor Orval Faubus attempted the first massive privatization of a city's public school system when he set up the Little Rock Private School Corporation. The Supreme Court ordered the schools reopened and integrated for all of 1958.

While the school system's desegregation was the end result, the goal on the part of the Little Rock Nine was simply, as Beals put it, "the best education possible."

"I wanted to go because students at Central had more privileges. They had more equipment; they had five floors of opportunity. I understood education before I understood anything else. From the time I was two, my mother said, 'You will go to college. Education is your key to survival.'"

Even after the horrendous example of Little Rock, countless other African-American women, men, boys, and girls would brave the threats to get a better education. History is filled with their stories—some well-known, some now forgotten. As the Little Rock Nine walked a gauntlet past a mob of angry whites, seventeen kids in Kentucky were facing flying rocks, cans, bottles, and fists, even dynamite, in order to register at all-white Sturgis High School. In Greensboro, North Carolina, five children were greeted with jeers and catcalls as they entered an all-white school. At the same time, schools in Clinton, Tennessee, began their second year of integrated classes without incident.[5]

## University of Alabama

On February 3, 1956, a year before Elizabeth Eckford and the rest of the Little Rock Nine endured their highly publicized ordeal, twenty-six-year-old Birmingham native Autherine Lucy was at the center of a firestorm of controversy. On that date, the young woman, described as modest and soft-spoken, with a ready smile, enrolled at the University of Alabama as a graduate student in library science. The applications of Lucy and a friend, Polly Ann Myers, made in 1952, were upheld by a federal court thanks to the efforts of NAACP lawyers, including Thurgood Marshall and Constance Baker Motley.[6]

For two years, the case worked its way through the courts. By the time federal judge Hobart H. Grooms ordered the university to admit the two women on July 1, 1955, Myers had married, given birth to a son, and was embroiled in a divorce. The University of Alabama trustees hastily seized on this as an excuse for rejecting her on "moral" grounds. Autherine Lucy alone braved the ensuing storm.

During the brief time Lucy attempted to attend classes as the first black in the university's 125-year history, crosses were burned on the campus. Police tried to control rampaging mobs of brick-throwing whites, shouting slogans like "Hey, ho, ho, Autherine must go," and "Keep 'Bama white." The uproar resulted in forty thousand whites joining the White Citizens' Council, a variation of the Ku Klux Klan. The price of miniature Confederate flags rose from fifteen to twenty-five cents and newspapers reported, "Parents Disown Miss Lucy's Fight." Even though sixty-nine-year-old Milton and Minnie Lucy denounced the youngest of their ten children, and pleaded with her to "come home to live with us or else go to some school that's all right for colored folks," others stood by her. One was Ruby Hurley, a regional director of the NAACP whose energy and enthusiasm would eventually expand that organization's membership in Alabama, Georgia, Florida, Mississippi, and Tennessee by tens of thousands. Hurley molded the organization's southeast region before becoming its director.

After less than a week, the university's board of trustees suspended Lucy "as a safety precaution." The NAACP lawyers filed a contempt of court suit against the university but failed to regain Lucy's admission to the University of Alabama.

Meanwhile, Lucy had moved to Texas, married her college sweetheart, the Reverend Hugh Foster, become the mother of five children, and worked as a teacher, before returning to Alabama in 1974. In 1988, sympathetic faculty convinced the University of Alabama's board to officially overturn Lucy's expulsion. One year later, Autherine Lucy Foster entered the University of Alabama to earn a master's degree in elementary education. In the spring of 1992, both she and her daughter, Grazia, received their degrees on the campus where her presence had once provoked riotous violence.[8]

## University of Georgia

The images of white viciousness that had tormented the nine youngsters trying to enter Little Rock's Central High School in 1957 were fresh in the minds of two young black people who began Atlanta's movement toward equality. Charlayne Hunter and Hamilton Holmes were the first blacks to enter the University of Georgia in 1959. The desire for a better education prompted the two honor students, who were at the top of their class, to make a bid to integrate the 176-year-old lily-white institution. A year after they filed their applications, a federal court order compelled the

*Charlayne Hunter*

university to admit them. Predictably, that order provoked the now-familiar round of cross-burnings, riots, and rumors that Governor Ernest Vandiver might keep a campaign promise to shut down the institution.

Years later, Hunter recalled journeying to the university's campus in Athens, Georgia, with an apprehensive convoy that included her mother, Hamilton Holmes's family, and a small team of NAACP lawyers. In her biography, *In My Place*, she remembers thinking about how she would take her first steps into this ivy-covered battlefield: "I found myself thinking about (a friend who walked with) a cool, confident stride that said, 'I love myself, and even if you don't love me, you will respect that which I love about myself.' That's how I would walk into the campus of Georgia, loving myself a lot and demanding respect."[6]

This determination bolstered Hunter when crowds of angry, taunting whites dogged her every footstep as she crossed the sprawling campus to register for classes. It also sustained her as crowds hovered outside her dormitory window at night, chanting, "Two, four, six, eight, we don't want to integrate...Eight, six, four, two, we don't want no jigaboo."

When protesters threw bricks through her first floor dormitory window before being dispersed by police tear gas, Hunter and Holmes, like Autherine Lucy, were spirited away in the wee hours of the night for their own safety. Rioting students supported by the Ku Klux Klan vowed to give Hunter and Holmes "the same greeting Autherine Lucy had gotten at the University of Alabama."

However, a federal court judge ordered the immediate reversal of their suspension by the University of Georgia, and they returned with armed, plainclothes government escorts. Even after things quieted down, Hunter, like Holmes, was forced to shoulder the heavy burden of being a symbol throughout college.

On June 1, 1963, Charlayne Hunter traveled once again from Atlanta to Athens, this time with a proud caravan of family and friends dressed in their Sunday-go-to-meeting best, to see her and Hamilton Holmes make history as two blacks in a graduating class of sixteen hundred—the first in the University of Georgia's history.

# 5

---

## MONTGOMERY BUS BOYCOTT:
## 1955–1956

On December 1, 1955, a seamstress, Rosa Parks, sitting in the black section of a Montgomery city bus, defied custom and refused to budge when the bus driver demanded she give up her seat for a white man. Today, practically every schoolchild has learned that Rosa Parks's refusal to relinquish her seat touched off the Montgomery bus boycott. The boycott began on December 5, 1955, as a one-day demonstration of blacks' dissatisfaction with the harassment by white bus drivers. When it ended on December 21, 1956, it had lasted 381 days and shaken the foundation of the South's "Jim Crow" segregation. The boycott led to a U.S. Supreme Court ruling that segregation on city buses was unconstitutional. It also catapulted into national prominence a twenty-six-year-old Baptist minister, Dr. Martin Luther King, Jr., and signaled the beginning of a mass movement of nonviolent resistance that would continue through the 1960s.

But many don't know that while Parks's courageous decision that December 1 might have been spontaneous, an army of women stood behind her and played a key role in getting the historic Montgomery bus boycott off the ground. The Women's Political Council (WPC), an organization of black professional women, was founded in 1946 by Mary Fair Burks, chair of the English department at Alabama State College. In 1955, she had just turned over the chair of the council to Jo Ann Robinson, an English professor at the same college.

With three chapters and a membership of some three hundred professional women—educators, social workers, nurses, and other community workers—it formed what Robinson called one of the best communication systems needed for operation of a boycott.[1]

Robinson says the WPC had been quietly planning a boycott of Montgomery City Lines for months. Horror stories of abuses suffered by blacks who rode Montgomery's buses were legion. A young black man was shot in the back by police after talking back to a bus driver in 1952. Two children visiting from New Jersy were arrested after refusing to give up their seat for a white man and boy. There was the tale of Mrs. Epsie Worthy who refused to pay an additional fare when the driver arbitrarily refused to take her transfer pass. She was arrested for disorderly conduct and fined fifty-two dollars because she defended herself when the driver started beating her. There was Jo Ann Robinson's own story of a Montgomery bus driver shouting at her and raising his fist as if to strike her when she unwittingly sat in the "whites only" section of a city bus only months after arriving in Montgomery.

Traditionally, of the bus's total thirty-six seats, the front ten double seats on each of the city's buses were reserved for whites, and could only be used by them. Even when all the seats were empty, blacks had to stand. Since the largest percentage of patrons of public transportation were black, one would often see the aisles crammed with black passengers of all ages, carrying children, bundles, or whatever, and standing over countless empty "reserved" seats that they dare not occupy.

There were other absurdities. Blacks had to enter the bus through the front door, put their money in the coin box, then get off and walk back and enter through the rear door to take their seat in the back of the bus. Sometimes white drivers would purposely drive off before black passengers who had paid could reenter the bus. While representatives of the bus lines often insisted that they were obeying the law in Alabama, many drivers frequently went out of their way to humiliate, berate, demean, and dehumanize their black passengers. Some operators snatched transfers from the hands of black passengers, or threw transfers or change in coins at them. Some refused to make change for blacks and accepted only exact fares. On rainy days black riders were "passed by" because white passengers did not want them standing over them.

The Women's Political Council had long monitored black passengers' complaints, searching for the ideal case for a boycott. For one brief moment months before the incident involving Rosa Parks, the perfect case seemed to be one involving a fifteen-year-old "A" student at Booker T. Washington High School—quiet, well-mannered, neat, clean, intelligent, pretty, and deeply religious Claudette Colvin.

On March 2, 1955, Colvin was sitting near the rear door of the bus when the driver told blacks to get up and give their seats to the white passengers as the bus had become crowded. Everyone did as they were told except Claudette. She refused even after police arrived and demanded that she get up, and then dragged her kicking and screaming off the bus. Handcuffed and hauled off to jail, she was charged with misconduct, resisting arrest, and violating the city segregation laws, and was held until her pastor bailed her out.

Word spread throughout the city. Montgomery's black community was a vast web of some sixty-eight organizations—political, religious, social, economic, educational, fraternal, and labor. There were groups of lawyers, doctors, educators, druggists, entertainers, musicians, farmers, builders, mechanics, maids, cooks, and more. Together, they touched every black man, woman, and child in Montgomery. All were active and capable of mobilizing the city's entire black population. They passed the word about Claudette Colvin, Robinson recalled, "yet we were not ready. Folks were not ready to boycott. They felt they had everything to lose and nothing to gain."[2]

Black leaders met with the city commissioner, the police, and the bus company manager, and came away believing the girl would be given "every fair chance to clear her name." But the tables were turned, and she was tried not under city law with its minor penalty, but under a stricter state law. She was found guilty and released on indefinite probation in her parents' care. Everyone was shocked.

"Intermittently, twenty to twenty-five thousand black people in Montgomery rode city buses," Robinson says, "and I would estimate that, up until the boycott of December 5, 1955, about three out of five had suffered some unhappy experience on the public transit lines. But the straw that broke the camel's back came on Thursday, December 1, 1955, when an incident occurred which was almost a repeat performance of the Claudette Colvin case."[3]

Rosa Parks boarded the bus during the busy evening rush hour and sat in one of the seats just behind a partially filled "reserved seats" section. When she twice refused the driver's demand that she get up and give her seat to a white man, police were summoned and for the first time in her life she was arrested and taken to jail.

Traditionally, Rosa Parks is portrayed simply as a weary, middle-aged seamstress who one day just got sick and tired and refused to give up her seat to a white person on a segregated bus. Actually, Rosa Louise McCauley Parks, a graduate of Alabama State College, was a youth adviser for the Montgomery NAACP and also served as the organization's secretary for twelve years. Her husband, Raymond Parks, had volunteered back in the 1930s to help free the Scottsboro Boys, black youths falsely accused of raping a white

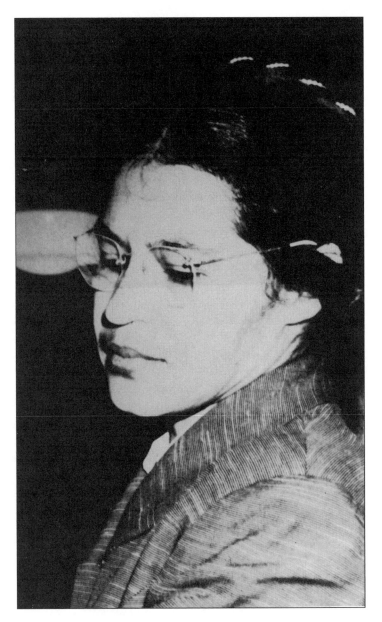

*Rosa Parks*

woman on a freight train. Just two months before, Rosa had spent a summer at the Highlander Folk School in Monteagle, Tennessee. The school was a well-known interracial training ground for labor leaders, where teachers and activists such as Septima Clark and Dorothy Cotton helped train generations of grassroots organizers.

The day of her arrest, Parks, who had "a life history of being rebellious against being mistreated because of my color," felt she had "been pushed as far as I could stand." She refused to move, she said, because "I was so involved with the attempt to bring about freedom from this kind of thing....I felt just resigned to give what I could to protest against the way I was being treated." She also felt, after years of involvement with quieter attempts to change things in Montgomery, that "all of our meetings, trying to negotiate, bring about petitions before authorities...really hadn't done any good at all."[4]

When word of her arrest reached them, E. D. Nixon, a longtime stalwart of the NAACP Montgomery branch; Fred Gray, a black defense attorney and ordained minister; liberal white attorney Clifford Durr, and his wife, Virginia, went to bail her out. Her trial was scheduled for Monday, December 5, 1955.

That night, when Jo Ann Robinson got a call from a young black lawyer, Fred Gray, she sprang into action. In the past, WPC officers had talked about how they would write and distribute notices announcing a bus boycott in the event one ever happened. Now Robinson was charged with carrying out these plans. Immediately, she wrote the following notice:

> *Another Negro woman has been arrested and thrown in jail because she refused to get up out of her seat on the bus for a white person to sit down. It is the second time since the Claudette Colvin case that a Negro woman has been arrested for the same thing. This has to be stopped. Negroes have rights, too, for if Negroes did not ride the buses, they could not operate. Three-fourths of the riders are Negroes, yet we*

*are arrested, or have to stand over empty seats. If we do not
do something to stop these arrests, they will continue. The
next time it may be you, or your daughter, or mother. This
woman's case will come up on Monday. We are, therefore,
asking every Negro to stay off the buses Monday in protest of
the arrest and trial. Don't ride the buses to work, to town, to
school, or anywhere on Monday. You can afford to stay out
of school for one day if you have no other way to go except by
bus. You can also afford to stay out of town for one day. If
you work, take a cab, or walk. But please, children and
grown-ups, don't ride the bus at all on Monday. Please stay
off all buses Monday.[5]*

Robinson did not get any sleep that night. Instead, she and
two students prepared the leaflets and followed a pre-
planned strategy to distribute thousands of leaflets so they
could reach every black home in Montgomery by the end of
the day. Twenty-two members of the WPC were notified,
and bundles were dropped off at prearranged pickup points.
Leaflets were also given to schools, businesses, storefronts,
beauty parlors, beer halls, factories, barber shops, and every
other available place. By early afternoon, the distribution of
52,500 mimeographed handbills had been so successful that
practially every black man, woman, and child in Montgomery knew the plan and was passing the word along.

Robinson is quick to credit the black clergy for the success of the Montgomery bus boycott, saying, "Had it not
been for the ministers and the support they received from
their congregations, the outcome of the boycott might have
been different." But all indications are that this is a very
humble assessment. The WPC was the initial force behind
the historic action. In fact, Montgomery's black clergy
learned about the action on December 2, 1955, just like
everyone else—from a bundle of leaflets Robinson had
printed and dropped off at the Hilliard Chapel AME Zion
Church during a meeting of the city's black ministers. The
ministers soon discovered that their congregations already
knew about the strike and were planning to support the

one-day boycott with or without the religious leaders' support. Robinson says, "The ministers decided that it was time for them, the leaders, to catch up with the masses." This they did as "for the first time in the history of Montgomery, black ministers—Baptist, Presbyterians, Episcopalians, Lutherans, Congregationalists—united to lead an action for civic improvement."[6]

Word of the boycott leaked out when one black woman domestic told her employer, who then tipped off the white newspaper, the *Alabama Journal.* Montgomery's afternoon newspaper printed the story, which was then picked up by two local television stations and four local radio stations. This did not stop the boycott.

An organizing meeting was held at the Dexter Avenue Baptist Church the Friday prior to December 5, to set up committees, designate responsibility, and develop a pickup system for walkers. Many have since admired the plan for its precision. The organizers also arranged a mass meeting for Monday night, at the largest black church in Montgomery, the Holt Street Baptist Church.

Monday morning, December 5, 1955, when buses "lumbered out of the Montgomery City Lines car shed and drove off in all directions to begin their rounds," Robinson recalled, "trailing each were two motorcycle policemen who had been assigned to follow buses into predominantly black areas 'to protect Negro riders' who would want to patronize the city transportation lines. Rumors had spread that hundreds of black domestics had telephoned their 'white folks' that they would not be at work on Monday because they were 'afraid to ride the bus.'"[7] This rumor, it appears, was designed to make it look like blacks were intimidated into supporting the boycott. Of course, Robinson said, there were no "goon squads" of blacks enforcing the boycott. Still, the boycott was 100 percent successful. All day long, empty buses moved down Montgomery's streets. Even very few white passengers rode the buses that day. Actually, 80 to 90 percent of those who traditionally rode the city buses were

A mass meeting to support the bus boycott in February 1956
in Montgomery, Alabama.

black. One bus driver reported that during his entire six-
hour run that day, he took in only six dollars and thirty
cents. The boycott had a domino effect, for downtown mer-
chants also lost money.

Monday night, six thousand black folks and local reporters packed the Holt Street Baptist Church for the first
of many mass meetings around the boycott. People spilled
out of the main auditorium, the overhanging balcony, the

basement, the aisles and steps, the front, side, and back yards and packed the three blocks up and down Holt Street. Amplifiers had been set up so people could hear, and although police patrolling the area warned those inside the church to turn down the volume, they kept it loud so all could hear what was going on inside.

That night, Montgomery people heard Reverend Ralph Abernathy pronounce the boycott a success, and praise the tremendous efforts of what was "not a one-man show, but the show of 45,000 black Montgomerians, and black Americans all over America and freedom-loving people everywhere." When asked whether to end the one-day boycott, thousands shouted a unanimous "NO!" Instead, the gathering voted to continue the boycott indefinitely and adopted a four-part resolution urging "All citizens of Montgomery to refrain from riding buses owned and operated by the City Lines Bus Company" until an agreement was reached. The people also declared that they were ready and willing to send a delegation to the bus company to discuss their grievances.

An organization was created that night which would lead the boycott—the Montgomery Improvement Association (MIA). A committee was appointed to draw up resolutions and to make proposals to be presented to the bus company. Dr. Martin Luther King, Jr., was elected president. King had recently arrived in town after receiving his Ph.D. in theology from Boston University. His father and grandfather had served as pastors of Atlanta's Ebenezer Baptist Church. Non-violent resistance was declared the doctrine by which their boycott would be conducted. Eight new officers, mainly ministers, filled every post from president to parliamentarian. There was only one woman among them—Mrs. Erna Dungee, the group's financial secretary. The executive board included Women's Political Council members Mrs. A. W. West, Sr., and Jo Ann Robinson. But despite this organization, the bulk of the decisions, right down to what money was supposed to be spent, was made by packed congregations that met every Monday at the Holt Street Church for the entire 381 days of the boycott.

The MIA's four paid staffers, charged with running the organization's day-to-day operation, were all women. In addition to Mrs. Dungee, who worked full-time the first six months of the boycott, there was Dr. King's personal secretary, Maude Ballou; a secretary-clerk, Martha Johnson; and the office manager, Hazel Gregory. Gregory managed the business, took care of the large five-room building MIA rented, and saw to it that it was locked securely at night. All of these women were also members of the WPC.

In order to keep the community informed throughout the boycott, a newsletter was produced by Robinson at the request of Dr. King. The English teacher from Alabama State, president of the WPC, and the woman whose leaflets had been largely responsible for the tremendous success of the boycott's first day, was now charged with gathering information, writing articles, and producing a publication. In addition to the nightly meetings at the Holt Street Baptist Church and black ministers' Sunday morning sermons, this newsletter was the primary source of information for the boycotters.

"I was attending each Monday night's MIA meeting and serving on the MIA executive board. It was no problem for me to take notes," Robinson recalls. "Then too, I served on a special Mayor's Committee, which handled our negotiations with city and bus company officials. I kept notes anyway, according to habit, and enjoyed it. Editing the MIA newsletter was nothing at all," she says.[8] Expenses were reimbursed, but Robinson and the other women never expected to and never did get paid.

Robinson relied on a network of sources to keep her informed, as well. The newsletter was four legal-sized pages, but soon after it came out, two pages had to be added, and before long it had to be enlarged again. Before the boycott was over, the MIA newsletter had grown to eight pages. As Dr. King had suggested, Robinson wrote the publication, then dropped it off at MIA headquarters for Dungee and Gregory to reproduce and send to a mailing list of thousands. Every family whose name was sent to Robinson received the letter, in addition to hundreds of folks outside Montgomery, in America and abroad.

"The plight of the Montgomery people was explained monthly in these pages and the national and even worldwide response was amazing. In a very short time, money was being mailed to MIA in large quantities. Any newsletter brought in thousands of dollars. The news items brought more. Thousands of dollars began to flow into MIA's treasury and did not cease for 13 months," Robinson says.[9]

The newsletters were an essential link in the communications system keeping boycotters and the outside world informed of the MIA's perspective on the lengthy, rocky negotiations process for the next thirteen months. Here, readers learned about the negotiations, which had been arranged after several days by a group of white ministers. Members of the Alabama Council on Human Relations, whose objective was to bring about better race relations, approached Mayor W. A. "Tacky" Gayle, the city's political leaders, the city's commissioners, and the bus company representatives, volunteering to arrange direct negotiations.

The newsletter published the demands presented by a special delegation headed by Dr. King. The delegation, which included other MIA leaders, two lawyers, and only two women, one of whom was Jo Ann Robinson, let them know what the demands were. If accepted, it would immediately end the boycott: "(1) Courtesy from bus drivers; (2) Negroes being able to sit from the rear toward the front and whites from the front toward the rear until all seats were taken. No one should have to surrender a seat once taken and no one would have to stand over an empty seat; and (3) Negro bus drivers be hired to operate buses on predominantly black routes." That was all.

Dr. King assured the press that the boycotters were not interested in changing present segregation laws, Robinson recalls, "but only wanted greater justice and better treatment for black people on the buses." The first of many negotiations, it lasted five hours and got nowhere.

In her account of the Montgomery bus boycott and the women who started it, Robinson says, "We did it for the specific purpose of finally integrating those buses. We were tired of second-class citizenship, tired of insults on buses from drivers who were cruel in order to make themselves appear big. The WPC wanted integration because of the abusive treatment of blacks on buses. We did not get up on the housetops to yell it and thus make our task even harder. For the sake of a peaceful fight, we kept silent on integration. We were not obnoxious about it, but quietly demanded it."[10] And, after months and months, they got it. But not without a fight.

# 6

## THE SIT-INS—SPRING 1960

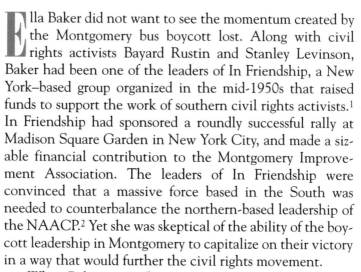

Ella Baker did not want to see the momentum created by the Montgomery bus boycott lost. Along with civil rights activists Bayard Rustin and Stanley Levinson, Baker had been one of the leaders of In Friendship, a New York–based group organized in the mid-1950s that raised funds to support the work of southern civil rights activists.[1] In Friendship had sponsored a roundly successful rally at Madison Square Garden in New York City, and made a sizable financial contribution to the Montgomery Improvement Association. The leaders of In Friendship were convinced that a massive force based in the South was needed to counterbalance the northern-based leadership of the NAACP.[2] Yet she was skeptical of the ability of the boycott leadership in Montgomery to capitalize on their victory in a way that would further the civil rights movement.

When Baker pointed out to Dr. Martin Luther King, Jr., that they needed a civil rights organization whose leadership had a southern base, she planted the seed that in January 1957 resulted in the founding of the Southern Christian Leadership Conference (SCLC) in Atlanta, Georgia. With Dr. King at its helm and Ella Baker the director of its Atlanta headquarters, SCLC mushroomed into sixty-five affiliates throughout the South. The SCLC was designed to allow black religious leaders to assume through the church the moral leadership of the civil rights movement. The church and its networks were the structural and psychological backbone of the black community. When Baker took on the task of running the day-to-day operations of SCLC's headquarters, she intended to stay on for just six weeks. She ended up shouldering this responsibility for two-and-a-half years.

SCLC was not the only civil rights organization to bear the distinct print of Ella Baker. Her drive, energy, and commitment to the civil rights struggle were remarkable, as was her ability to help folks shape their political future. Throughout her eighty years, Baker was affiliated with close to fifty organizations and coalitions. She served as everything, from founder to foot soldier, from the 1930s to her death in 1986. True to the tradition of Ida B. Wells, Mary Church Terrell, and Mary McLeod Bethune, Baker left an indelible mark on twentieth-century American political history.

At the time SCLC was founded, Baker already had an impressive track record. Her fiercely democratic spirit had been shaped by the close-knit North Carolina black community of her youth that was held together by a web of mutual cooperation and extended family ties. She had also been affected by the swirling cauldron of progressive politics energizing Harlem, where she moved after graduating from Shaw University in Raleigh, North Carolina. Baker's involvements with a series of groups made her one of the most influential organizers in the civil rights movement.

Baker first joined the Young Negroes Cooperative League (YNCL), which organized, throughout the Northeast and Midwest, consumer buying clubs, a restaurant, cooperative grocery stores, cooperative distribution networks, and even a housing development. In 1931, she became the group's first national director. During the Roosevelt years, she was part of the massive Worker's Education Project of

*Ella Baker*

the Works Progress Administration. Her interest in the fight for women's equality prompted her to support groups as diverse as the Women's Day Workers and the Industrial League—a union of domestic workers—and the Harlem YWCA.

In the 1940s, Baker became a field secretary with the NAACP. Here, she honed her skills as an organizer and learned more about the inner workings and failures of the established civil rights movement. She also developed a grassroots network, a "web of contacts in the South," that would prove indispensable. Later, Baker served as director of the branches from 1943 to 1946, and then as president of the New York City branch in 1954, the first woman to hold that post. During this time, Baker campaigned to create accessible channels through which local people could participate more fully in the NAACP.

As head of a group called Parents against Discrimination in Education, Baker fought for the desegregation of New York City's public schools and greater parental involvement in school decision-making. Baker also made a lone foray into electoral politics by throwing her hat into the 1951 race for a seat on the New York City Council.

Baker believed strongly in empowering people to shape their own future. She realized after she joined the SCLC staff that the heavy reliance on King's charisma to mobilize people would eventually undermine the organizing of the civil rights movement. Baker was also aware that, because she was a woman, SCLC's male leadership did not give her the recognition she deserved.

"You didn't see me on television, you didn't see news stories about me," she boasted, explaining her strong position against the cult of personality. "The kind of role that I tried to play was to pick up pieces or put together pieces out of which I hoped organization might come. My theory is strong people don't need strong leaders."[3]

The opportunity to prove her point came soon after the first student-led sit-in at Greensboro, North Carolina, on February 1, 1960. The sit-in revealed a new level of protest and inspired Ella Baker to help form a new type of civil rights organization, the Student Non-violent Coordinating Committee (SNCC). When three black students from North Carolina Agricultural and Technical College decided to sit down at a segregated lunch counter in a local five-and-dime store, and vowed to remain until they were served, they started something that swept through the South like a brushfire through a field of dry grass. Lunch counters in five-and-dime stores were as much a symbol of the inanity of America's system of petty apartheid as "reserved" seating in public buses. Like these other symbols, they were inhumane and humiliating daily reminders of the belief that blacks were inferior to whites. When the four students dared to sit-in at the Greensboro lunch counter, they were launching an attack at the public face of apartheid while also sparking a movement.

According to historian Harvard Sitkoff, by April 1960, the tactic had spread to sixty-eight southern and border communities, and some two thousand students had been arrested. A year later, in September 1961, at least seventy thousand blacks and whites had actively participated in the massive wave of sit-ins against unjust laws and Jim Crow practices. The students had taken action because they had grown disenchanted with the slow pace of the struggle being led by the older, more established civil rights organizations.[4]

Historian Howard Zinn remembers, "In a matter of days, the sit-in idea leaped to other cities. During the next two weeks, sit-ins spread to fifteen cities in five southern states. Within the following year, over fifty thousand people — most were Negroes, some were white — had participated in one kind of demonstration or another in a hundred cities, and over 3,600 demonstrators spent time in jail. But there were results to show: by the end of 1961, several hundred lunch counters had been desegregated in scores of cities—in Texas, Oklahoma, the border states of the South, and even as far away as Atlanta, Georgia. A wall of resistance, however, apparently impenetrable, faced students in the rest of Georgia, South Carolina, Alabama, Mississippi, Louisiana—the hard-core, Deep South."[5]

Televised accounts of the sit-ins inspired young college students throughout the country. Ruby Doris Smith, a sev-

*A sit-in*

enteen-year-old sophomore at Spellman College, recalled
seeing the Greensboro sit-in on television:

> I began to think right away about it happening in Atlanta, but
> I wasn't ready to act on my own. When the student commit-
> tee was formed in the Atlanta University Center, I told my

*older sister, who was on the Student Council at Morris Brown College, to put me on the list. And when 200 students were selected for the first demonstration, I was among them. I went through the food line in the restaurant at the State Capitol with six other students, but when we got to the cashier, she wouldn't take our money. She ran upstairs to get the Governor. The Lieutenant-Governor came down and told us to leave. We didn't and went to the county jail.[6]*

Ruby Doris Smith would soon join the army of young college students—many of them women—whose commitment and energy would revitalize the civil rights movement. Smith would rise from the ranks to become one of the movement's legendary leaders—a bold, daring, hardworking, dedicated woman who demanded as much as she gave from everyone around her. Smith devoted her life to the movement until she died of cancer at the young age of twenty-five. James Foreman, head and founder of the Congress of Racial Equality, described her as one of the few genuine revolutionaries in the black liberation movement.

The sit-ins required a tremendous amount of courage and discipline, for while the first sit-in by four students in Greensboro was without incident, it did not take long before sit-in demonstrators met with opposition. Angry, ugly mobs sneeringly shouted racial epithets like "nigger" to blacks, and "nigger-lover" to whites while jamming lighted cigarettes against the backs of boys and girls alike. Racists yanked demonstrators off the stools, spitting and punching and kicking and hitting them, as others, including police, looked on. Eventually the police arrested only the demonstrators. The same extralegal forms of terrorism that southerners had used for centuries to reinforce slavery and oppression of blacks were now acted out before television cameras and newspaper reporters. The photographs inflamed passions on both sides of the argument and showed the courage and determination of those who joined the ranks of this new American Revolution.

Howard Zinn reports that a "white sit-in student was attacked in jail and his jaw broken, a sixteen-year-old black boy was pistol-whipped by the Ku Klux Klan, a Negro unconnected with the demonstrations who went through a police roadblock was shot to death by a white service-station attendant. In Atlanta, acid was thrown at sit-in leader Lonnie King. In Frankfort, Kentucky, the gymnasium of a Negro college was set on fire. In Columbia, South Carolina, a Negro sit-in student was stabbed. In Houston, Texas, a twenty-seven-year-old was kidnapped and flogged with a chain, and the symbol of the KKK was carved on his chest. In one southern city, police used clubs, tear gas, and police dogs against students. Women, children, and a photographer were bitten by dogs. In Biloxi, Mississippi, Negroes trying to use public beaches were attacked with clubs and chains by a crowd of whites, and ten were wounded by gunfire."[7]

One by one the future leaders of this new wave of activists were inspired by the sit-ins. John Lewis, now a congressional representative from Georgia and one of the future leaders, recalled "feeling that we were involved in something like a crusade. It was a sense of duty, you had an obligation to do it, to redeem the soul of America."[8]

Diane Nash, a tiny, slender, campus beauty queen at Fisk, one of the pillars of the Nashville student sit-in movement, was inspired by the Greensboro incident. Twelve days after Greensboro, she and student leaders John Lewis and Julian Bond lead some forty students in a sit-in at Woolworth's in Nashville, igniting a spark that would stun that city. An ever-increasing army of protesters grew to four thousand when blacks marched through the streets to city hall after the bombing of the home of defense lawyer Z. Alexander Looby. There, Nash confronted Nashville's mayor on the steps of city hall:

> We needed him to say integrate the counters, to tell Nashville to do what Nashville knew it should have done a long time ago. I asked the mayor, "Mayor Webster do you feel it is immoral to discriminate against a person solely on the basis of his race or color?" West said, "I have to agree that I do not

*think it is right for someone to sell them merchandise, then refuse them service."*[9]

Nash's question, and the mayor's frank and honest answer, were the turning point in the Nashville battle. Three weeks later, blacks were served for the first time at lunch counters in downtown stores. Nash, who was chair of the Student Central Committee in Nashville, which organized sit-ins at Woolworth's, Walgreen's, Kress, and two department stores, would go on to attend the historic founding meeting of the Student Non-violent Coordinating Committee in Raleigh, North Carolina.

While the sit-ins were spreading throughout the South, Ella Baker saw the need for some sort of coordination and structure. "I suggested that we call a conference of the sit-iners to be held in Raleigh. It was very obvious to the Southern Christian Leadership Conference that there was little or no communication between those who sat in, say, in Charlotte, North Carolina, and those who eventually sat in at some other place in Virginia or Alabama. They were motivated by what the North Carolina four had started, but they were not in contact with each other, which meant that you couldn't build a sustaining force just based on spontaneity," Baker later told an interviewer.[10]

Baker persuaded SCLC to donate eight hundred dollars and her alma mater, Shaw University, to contribute its campus. The conference was much more successful than she had anticipated. When the Youth Leadership Meeting convened on April 15, 1960, instead of the expected few young leaders of the campus sit-ins, there were three hundred people.

The sit-ins reflected the mood of impatience of the young. They could recall their parents' jubilant reaction six years earlier to the *Brown v. Board of Education* decision, and they remembered the riveting images of Elizabeth Eckford as she made her way through fierce, angry mobs outside Little Rock's Central High School. Despite these dramatic indications that the system of segregation was being dismantled, the youths still confronted the immediate signs of its intransigence: segregated lunch counters, segregated water fountains, and more. To them, it was time for a change, and rather than wait for someone else to make change happen, they took it upon themselves. Sit-ins at lunch counters were joined by sit-ins at restaurants and at movies, kneel-ins at churches, wade-ins at pools and beaches, and a dozen different kinds of extralegal demonstrations against segregation.

The message of these forms of protest was all too clear. They were more than just demonstrations, they were portents of a changing attitude toward participatory democracy. Sit-ins and other forms of nonviolent civil disobedience, as well as protest marches—hallmarks of the civil rights movement—would have far-reaching implications as they became the weapon of choice used by protesters in countless demonstrations in the decades that followed. After the 1963 March on Washington, the sight of thousands, even millions, rallying on the stretch of lawn between the Washington Monument and the Lincoln Memorial was not unusual. The forms of protest popularized by civil rights activists became the backbone of the actions taken by Vietnam war protesters, women demanding equal rights, gay rights activists, and even AIDS activists.

The student movement galvanized the older organizations into a new dynamism, and won the support of some of the established black leaders, who quickly sensed that a new wind was blowing. The student movement left far behind those leaders who could not break either old habits of thinking, or old ties with the white elite. Ella Baker was one of those leaders who realized, before anyone else, just how important those demonstrations were.

Baker delivered the conference's opening address, "More Than a Hamburger," to student delegates from fifty-six colleges in twelve southern states, as well as students and observers from nineteen northern schools. Baker applauded the students' "inclination toward group-centered leadership, rather than toward a leader-centered group pattern of organization" as refreshing "to those of the older group who bear the scars of the battle, the frustrations and disillusionment that come when the prophetic leader turns out to have heavy feet of clay."[11] She had championed their independence behind the scenes, too, at one organization meeting during the conference.

> *The Southern Christian Leadership Conference felt that they could influence how things went. They were interested in having the students become an arm of SCLC. They were confident that this would be their baby because I was their functionary and I had called the meeting. At a discussion called by the Rev. Dr. King, the SCLC leadership decided who would speak to whom to influence the students to become part of the SCLC. Well, I disagreed. There was no student at Dr. King's meeting. I was the nearest thing to a student, being the advocate, you see. I also knew from the beginning that having a woman be an executive of SCLC was not something that would go over with the male-dominated leadership. And, then, of course, my personality wasn't right, in the sense that I was not afraid to disagree with the higher authorities. I wasn't one to say, yes, because it came from the Rev. King. So, when it was proposed that the leadership could influence the direction by speaking to, let's say, the man from Virginia, who could speak to the leadership of the Virginia student group, and the assumption was that having spoken to so-and-so, so-and-so would do what they wanted done, I was outraged. I walked out.[12]*

Dr. King also addressed the students. He recommended an organization to coordinate the student struggle, a nationwide campaign of "selective buying" to punish segregating variety-store chains, and an army of volunteers who would willingly go to jail rather than pay bail or fines. His emphasis on the tactics and spirit of nonviolence touched off a controversy. In the end, the students clearly decided that nonviolence was purely a political weapon and a tactical move, and nothing more, and they rebuked the NAACP and SCLC for their lack of aggressive militancy.

The group elected Marion Barry of Nashville as its chairman, although many believed that Diane Nash, the chair of the Student Central Committee of Nashville, would have been selected had she not come late to the meeting. Nonetheless, Nash would go on to be one of the leaders and driving forces of SNCC.

During the conference, which lasted from April 16 to 18, the group established a temporary coordinating committee. A month later it met with SCLC's Baker and a leader of the Congress of Racial Equality (CORE), and voted not to be affiliated with any other group; they would remain an independent organization called the Temporary Student Nonviolent Coordinating Committee. At the plenary conference later that same year, "Temporary" would be dropped from the name. At that meeting, the new SNCC chairman, Charles McDrew, made the group's goal perfectly clear: "The sit-ins have inspired us to build a new image of ourselves in our own minds. And, instead of sitting idly by, taking the leavings of a sick and decadent society, we have seized the initiative, and already the walls have begun to crumble." He added that the movement would not end "until every vestige of racial segregation and discrimination are erased from the face of the earth."

Nash has described Ella Baker's role. "Ella Baker was very important in giving direction to the student movement. Not giving direction in a way of making her decisions in terms of what the students ought to do, but in terms of really seeing how important it was to recognize that the students should set the goals and directions and maintain control of the student movement."[13]

With this as their purpose, the students, with the help of Ella Baker, set about clearing away the vestiges of segregation.

# 7

## THE FREEDOM RIDES
## 1960–1961

A "buzzing jumble of rooms," is how one observer described SNCC's headquarters above a tailor shop in the black section of Atlanta, Georgia. From this central command post the two chief officers with the help of a handful of office staffers; an adviser, Ella Baker; and a network of field secretaries scattered throughout the South coordinated the rash of demonstrations of 1960. It wasn't easy. Not only did the group operate on a shoestring while awaiting promised money from churches, colleges, foundations, and fund-raisers, but the sit-ins had acquired their own momentum, and trying to coordinate them was a bit like trying to tame a tornado. The winds of change were blowing, and just where the next storm would strike was anybody's guess. The organization operated on a paltry budget of fourteen thousand dollars, with more than three-fourths of its forty field workers under twenty-two years of age and burning with idealism and impatience. One leader was Bob Moses, a young black Harvard graduate student who had taught mathematics at the Horace Mann School in New York City. SNCC operated on the principle articulated by Moses: "Go where the spirit say go and do what the spirit say do."

According to one SNCC staffer, Joan Wiley, everyone was his or her own leader to some extent. Those who took it upon themselves to do something, generally did it. This spirit has been described as fertile ground for the development of female leadership. "Both the structural nature and the goals of SNCC propelled women into the forefront of the struggle in a way that was not possible in more hierarchical male-led organizations," writes historian Paula Giddings.

Many of these young girls had "female doers as role models," whether their own mothers had histories of political activity or they had seen other black women in activist roles. Certainly their mothers worked and were usually capable of coping with any situation that could affect their children's lives. Angela Davis, who joined SNCC in California in the mid-1960s, was the daughter of Sallie Bell Davis, who had been one of the Birmingham leaders of the Student Southern Negro Youth Congress. Sallie Bell Davis had participated in college in the campaign to free the Scottsboro Boys, and later remained associated with the Birmingham NAACP after it was banned by authorities in the mid-1950s. SNCC staffer Jean Smith's mother always told her, "I could do anything I was big enough to do."[1] With this spirit and their uncompromising zeal, the young women of SNCC could move mountains—and they did.

Few of these women thought themselves incapable of doing anything men could do, including facing physical danger. In fact, some have insisted that SNCC became the most dynamic and progressive organization in the history of the civil rights movement because black women were such an integral part of it. They were enthusiastic college coeds, like Diane Nash, who had led sit-in movements; they were residents of the southern towns and backwaters where SNCC staffers set up shop, like Gloria Richardson Dandridge of Cambridge, Maryland, or Fannie Lou Hamer of Ruleville, Mississippi. Many would go on to become legendary leaders in their own right.

In February 1961, eleven students who were arrested

during a sit-in demonstration in Rock Hill, South Carolina elected to refuse to pay bail and go to jail. Their actions reflected a bold new attack conceived, some say, by Diane Nash. Nash, Ruby Doris Smith, and nine male SNCC volunteers served thirty days of hard labor. Soon their "jail-no-bail" tactic swept through the South.

When Nash was jailed in Mississippi, four months pregnant (she had married SNCC staffer James Bevel a year earlier), she opted to remain in jail rather than appeal her conviction. "We in the nonviolent movement have been talking about jail without bail for two years or more," she said. "The time has come for us to mean what we say and stop posting bond. This will be a black baby born in Mississippi and thus, wherever it is born, it will be born in prison. I believe that if I go to jail now it will help hasten that day when my child and all children will be free—not only on the day of their birth but for all their lives."[2]

That same uncompromising attitude carried the young women and men (who were now the vanguard of the civil rights movement) through the next phase of the struggle. The spring and summer of 1961 brought yet another breeze of fresh air to blow away the cobwebs of antiquated southern customs: the Freedom Rides. Whatever else they were, the Freedom Rides were not free and the youthful volunteers paid their dues.

James Farmer, the new national director of the Congress of Racial Equality, issued a call on March 13, 1961, for volunteers to conduct "Freedom Rides" through the South. The purpose was to force compliance with the Supreme Court ruling that prohibited segregation in vehicles engaged in interstate travel as well as in all their terminals. Farmer was taking a page out of CORE's own history. CORE had initiated nonviolent direct action against racial discrimination with its 1947 "Journey of Reconciliation," a campaign designed by civil rights activist Bayard Rustin. In 1947 their ride through the South had been relatively quiet, with little violence and few arrests, and scant attention

*A bus with freedom riders is set afire in Anniston, Alabama.*

from the national press. This would not be the case with the 1961 Freedom Rides, which were designed to compel the President to enforce the Supreme Court decisions prohibiting segregation in vehicles that travelled across state lines—decisions that the South had largely ignored. The Kennedy administration had the power, through the Interstate Commerce Commission, to force the states to obey the law. Farmer said, "We decided the way to do it was to have a

*Freedom riders arrive in New Orleans by plane. (Left to right) David Dennis, Julia Aaron, Jerome H. Smith, and Doris Castle.*

group ride through the South...whites sitting at the back of the bus, blacks at the front. At every rest stop, whites would go into the waiting room for blacks, and the blacks into the waiting room for whites. We felt we could count on the racists to create a crisis so that the federal government would be compelled to enforce federal law."[3]

Starting in Washington, D.C., the "freedom riders" encountered only minor resistance in the upper South. Then on Mother's Day, May 14, their Greyhound bus curved along U.S. Highway 78 and pulled into Anniston, Alabama. An angry mob was waiting armed with blackjacks, iron bars, clubs, and tire chains, with which people smashed windows and slashed tires. Next, they firebombed the bus, which burst into flames, leaving only a charred metal skeleton. Fortunately, the riders escaped from the bus. Local hospital personnel, however, refused to treat the freedom riders who had been cut by flying glass and overcome by smoke inhalation. It took an armed caravan of cars from Birmingham, Alabama, led by Reverend Fred Shuttlesworth, to get the freedom riders out of town.

The second vehicle, a Trailways bus, pulled into Anniston one hour later. The mob jumped aboard and beat the riders mercilessly, leaving one sixty-one-year-old retired teacher, Walter Bergman, permanently brain damaged and close to death. This was only the beginning of the violence the freedom riders, both men and women, black and white, would experience. When the buses arrived in Birmingham, Alabama, yet another angry mob of whites was waiting. Police were nowhere in sight, even though Commissioner Eugene "Bull" Connor's headquarters was only two blocks away. Cops didn't arrive until the group of Ku Klux Klan goons had left. Although one rider had been beaten unconscious and required fifty-three stitches, the group wanted to continue, but the bus drivers refused to go any further. Air travel to New Orleans for the riders was specially arranged by the Justice Department.

At this point, CORE even contemplated calling off the Freedom Rides. When SNCC leader Diane Nash got word of what had happened, she leaped into action along with other SNCC volunteers who believed the rides should go on. "We felt that even if we had to do it ourselves, the Freedom Rides had to continue," said Lucretia Collins, a Tennessee State coed who had left school just weeks before her graduation to join the rides. "We knew we were subject to

*Soldiers guard a bus carrying freedom riders.*

being killed. This did not matter to us. There was so much at stake, we could not allow the segregationists to stop us."[4]

Many of the SNCC volunteers who went on the rides made out wills, and gave Nash notes and sealed letters to be mailed in the event of their death. In fact, one of the training questions volunteers were routinely asked was simply, "Are you prepared to die?" Every young woman and man who boarded a Freedom Ride bus knew that they were putting their lives on the line and they did so freely, willingly, and with a degree of enthusiasm that left many in awe.

"If the Freedom Rides had been stopped because of violence," Nash said, "I strongly felt that the future of the movement was going to be cut short. The impression would have been given that whenever a movement starts all that had to be done was meet it with massive violence and the blacks would stop."[5]

In those early months, the freedom rides encountered yet more violence. Their buses were firebombed, and reluctant southern authorities offered only scant protection. The federal government, under the newly elected President John Kennedy and his brother, Attorney General Robert Kennedy, was drawn increasingly into the fray. While campaigning, President Kennedy had taken several highly publicized stands in support of the civil rights activists that encouraged black ministers to endorse him from the pulpit the Sunday before election day. This brought out the record black vote that gave Kennedy the narrow margin of victory he needed to win against Richard Nixon. An incredibly tense standoff took place between over twelve hundred blacks, including the freedom riders and Dr. Martin Luther King, Jr., who were barricaded in a Montgomery church, and a violent crowd of whites outside. The Alabama governor was forced to call in the National Guard rather than have the Feds act. The Kennedy administration and even some civil rights leaders called for a cooling-off period, which the SNCC leaders resisted.

Instead, the Freedom Rides continued unabated, pushing deeper and deeper into the South, where the fuzzy link between the Ku Klux Klan, White Citizens Councils, and the established order had allowed terror to reign. In Mississippi, the riders were arrested and put in Parchman State Penitentiary, a maximum security prison. Ruby Doris Smith was one of over three hundred people who endured the indignities of the prison's strip search, and the filthy, insect-infested cells containing little more than a mattress.

When the riders began to sing freedom songs (which they did all the time), towels and toothbrushes were confiscated. Even sheets and mattresses were taken away. Some prisoners were subjected to battery operated cattle-prodders and wrist-breakers. Roughneck prison guards with faces contorted by hate and the epithet "nigger" on the tip of their tongues would have just as soon killed them as look at them. But the freedom riders' spirits remained high. They embraced prison with a messianic zeal, for after all, they were on a crusade. As James Farmer said: "Jails were not a new experience for the riders, but the freedom riders were definitely a new experience for Mississippi jails."[6] Even as that group of freedom riders went to prison, hundreds more poured into the southern states. On September 22, 1961, at the urging of the Kennedy administration, the Interstate Commerce Commission reinforced the Supreme Court's mandate against racial discrimination on interstate buses and bus facilities.

While all this was going on, the future of the movement was being determined by SNCC leaders in meetings at the Highlander Folk School in Tennessee. Some of the meetings were also attended by representatives of the Kennedy administration's Justice Department. In an attempt to redirect the movement and end direct actions and the violent confrontations, the Justice Department encouraged the movement to focus on voter registration, an activity it believed to be less provocative. SNCC was urged to move voter registration to the top of its agenda. Coupled with the Kennedy administration's call for a cooling-off period for the Freedom Rides, this sparked a heated controversy during one Highlander meeting as the voter registration proposal was pitted against the direct action approach, which had given birth to the sit-ins and the Freedom Rides. Ella Baker suggested a compromise that would allow both to continue and the movement to flourish as it headed into the arena of electoral politics: SNCC would have two arms—one, under the direction of Diane Nash, would focus on direct action projects; the other, under the direction of Charles Jones, would be devoted to voter registration. SNCC would be able to continue dismantling Jim Crow laws and America's system of petty apartheid and, at the same time, move to the core of political power to change the complexion of Congress. More important, women would be in the forefront of both efforts, as well as beneficiaries of the results in the decades to come.

# 8

## IN THE STREETS
## 1961–1964

The role of black women as the backbone of the civil rights movement was reflected in the lives of countless heroines. Some will be remembered by millions for generations to come, and others will be largely forgotten. As Ella Baker said, the number of women who carried the movement is much larger than that of men. Seeking explanations, some have pointed to the role of the black church, the most cohesive institution in the Deep South, capable of reaching large segments of the black populace. As one historian has pointed out, "The movement of the fifties and sixties was carried largely by women since it came out of the church groups."[1]

Modern-day Sojourner Truths is what historian Paula Giddings called the women who opened up their homes and hearts to the SNCC volunteers who came to convince blacks to register to vote. Mary Dora Jones, who was told that her house would be burned down if she continued to insist on putting up the SNCC workers, said, "Dyin' is all right. Ain't but one thing 'bout dyin'. That's make sho' you right, 'cause you gonna die anyway. If they had burned it down, it was just a house burned down."[2]

SNCC worker Joan Wiley recalls that these black

women carried the necessary moral and social authority when difficult decisions had to be made. On numerous occasions ministers not wanting to open their churches to the civil rights workers did so only after the women insisted. SNCC worker Charles Sherrod recalled, "There is always a 'mama'; she is usually a militant woman in the community, outspoken, understanding, and willing to catch hell, having already caught her share."

## The Cambridge Movement

Some of these women became leaders in their own right. In the 1960s the civil rights movement came to Gloria Richardson Dandridge's hometown of Cambridge, Maryland. The Cambridge Movement was unique. It was the first grassroots effort outside the Deep South and one of the first to take on a very militant tone. It was also one of the first to protest economic injustice.

In Cambridge blacks had been voting since 1869 and Dandridge's grandfather, H. Maynadier St. Clair, had served on the council from 1912 to 1946. The unemployment rate was almost 50 percent in the predominantly black Second Ward, the highest in the state, three times that of Cambridge's white community and six times that of the nation. Many blacks were earning less than $3,000 a year. Economic issues were bound to hit home.

The movement for change began in 1961. Students from Harvard, Howard, Dandridge's alma mater, Maryland State, Swarthmore, Morgan State, and other colleges came to town under the auspices of the Student Nonviolent Coordinating Committee. Dandridge recalls, "At first it was these kids from out of state who were coming in to stir things up. I got to know them because of my daughter Donna's involvement with them.

"There was something direct, real, about the way the kids waged nonviolent war. This was the first time I saw a vehicle I could work with. With SNCC, there was not all of the red tape—you just got things done. Before I knew it I was one of the leaders. That first spring, SNCC was there having the church meetings and rallies. We were trying to coordinate and cooperate with the NAACP, such as it was in Cambridge."[3]

Before long, a new group, the Cambridge Nonviolent Action Committee (CNAC), was formed with Gloria Richardson Dandridge as its leader. Its weekly meetings took place in the building where Dandridge's father's pharmacy was once located. Because of SNCC's unique structure, affiliation with the national civil rights group did not undermine the local group's autonomy.

While the group participated in voter registration drives, the committee's primary focus was on a host of economic problems plaguing the impoverished community—inadequate housing, underfunded educational facilities, poor health care, and the lack of jobs.

In 1963 the heat was turned up when Dandridge led CNAC's sit-ins protesting segregated seating in the Dorset Theatre. Soon they targeted other public accommodations. On one occasion Dandridge's daughter was arrested during a protest in the Dorset Theater lobby while Dandridge and her mother, Mabel St. Clair Booth, were arrested at a protest at the Dizzyland Restaurant. All three found themselves in the same crowded jail. At a show trial the judge fined eighty activists a penny, gave them suspended sentences, and lectured Dandridge on how she was disgracing her family's name.

Keeping the pressure on, persistent protesters forced the city political leaders to agree to several demands: desegregation of public places and public schools; equal employment opportunities in industry and stores; construction of a public housing project; and an end to police brutality.

The tenuous peace was soon shattered when two young people were sentenced for their part in several demonstrations. Violent confrontations raged during the summer of 1963. State police, armed with riot sticks and attack dogs,

*Gloria Richardson Dandridge*

were rushed in, and martial law was eventually declared. Dandridge appealed to Attorney General Robert Kennedy to intervene. Governor Townes called in the Maryland National Guard after more violent confrontations between black protesters and white protesters.

In late July, Dandridge and a group of civil rights leaders were invited to Washington to find a solution.

She recalls: "We carried our demands to Robert Kennedy, all the things we knew could be resolved. John Lewis came. The leaders all had been in and out of Cambridge, cause there had been massive demonstrations when Governor Wallace was there. Leaders came in from all over, not only from SNCC but from up and down the East Coast. James Foreman, Bill Savage, and Stanley Branch came from the national office of the NAACP." The male leaders seemed to dominate the meeting, but Dandridge changed that: "At one point I had to tell Robert Kennedy that nobody here can speak for Cambridge except those of us from the Cambridge Nonviolent Action Committee, so you can forget what the rest are saying."

Dandridge credits Kennedy's insistence for the fact that Governor Townes of Maryland and the mayor of Cambridge finally signed the five-point Treaty of Cambridge.

The treaty called for complete and immediate desegregation of public schools and hospitals, construction of 200 units of low-income public housing for blacks, employment of a black in the Cambridge office of Employment Security and in the post office, the appointment of a Human Relations Commission, and the adoption of a Charter Amendment that provided for desegregation of public accommodations.

The Charter Amendment was subjected to a referendum despite Dandridge's strong objections. With half of the black voters boycotting the polls, the referendum lost by 274 votes. Dandridge asserted that equality was a moral question, not one to be voted up or down by the electorate. Dandridge came under considerable fire for this stand from black male leaders in the civil rights movement, including Martin Luther King, Jr.

Afterwards, things in Cambridge, Maryland changed slowly. The National Guard remained in Cambridge through 1963 and the first half of 1964. Attorney General Robert Kennedy announced an on-the-job training program for one hundred blacks in Cambridge to be administered under the Manpower Development Act. This was "a long-sought goal of Dandridge who had presaged the War on Poverty view that economic oppression was just as wrong as civil injustice."[3]

Demonstrations continued almost until July 1964, when President Lyndon Baines Johnson signed the Civil Rights Act, forcing the integration of the Dorset Theater, Dizzyland, Coney Lanes Bowling Alley, and other public accommodations.

Another town where women grassroots activists would take up the mantle of leadership was Albany, Georgia.

## The Albany Movement

In May of 1961, the movement launched a struggle in the tiny southwest Georgia town of Albany that would become the first nationally covered civil rights struggle since the Freedom Rides. With its unprecedented mass arrests, Albany was called by some historians the first large-scale uprising since the Montgomery bus boycott, and women were once again on the front lines.

Their efforts sparked a new direction in the movement. The heavy reliance on grassroots organizing and local activists helped develop a new type of demonstration. According to SNCC historian Howard Zinn, "Albany represented a permanent turn from the lunch counter and the bus terminal to the streets, from hit-and-run attacks by students and professional civil rights workers to populist rebellion by lower-class Negroes."[4]

In this town in the heart of the "Black Belt," blacks made up 40 percent of the population of fifty-six thousand. They lived in a society segregated from cradle to grave. Albany had also been the trading center for the slave plantation country of southwest Georgia. Segregation had a stranglehold on the people's psyche, and SNCC's task was to try and pry it loose. SNCC staffers, twenty-two-year-old Charles Sherrod and eighteen-year-old Cordell Reagan, had arrived in town to set up a voter registration office. At first, many of the ministers were afraid to let the SNCC volunteers use their churches, for they were afraid the churches would be bombed and their homes would be stoned. Despite this climate of fear, a few brave souls ventured to help. One was Irene Asbury Wright, dean of students at Albany State College for Negroes. When the SNCC organizers began speaking to the students about voter registration, they encountered the resistance of the president of the conservative black college. He didn't want to offend the body that oversaw the school's finances—the white Board of Regents of the State of Georgia. Irene Wright resigned in protest against the administration's repressive policies and opened her home to the activists.

The SNCC activists held role-playing workshops for nonviolent protest. As things began to stir, they attracted an army of young people from the colleges, trade schools, and high schools and from the street. A date had been set for the implementation of the Interstate Commerce Commission ruling that barred segregation in terminals. This impending date, and the group's own sense of urgency, made it clear that it was time to act.

Wright was one of the forces behind the creation of the Albany Movement, a coalition of the NAACP Youth Council, the Baptist Ministers Alliance, and other groups that joined with SNCC. Wright said the need to move was clear: "The kids were going to do it anyway...they were holding their own mass meetings and making plans; we didn't want them to have to do it alone."[5]

On the weekend before the Thanksgiving holiday, the students decided to test the ICC ruling. Albany police chief Laurie Pritchett, a diehard segregationist whom the Albany action would show to be a clever strategist, arrested Bertha Gober of Atlanta when she, along with another Albany State student, entered the terminal's white waiting room.

After her arrest, Bertha Gober was suspended from Albany State. Another Albany State activist who was suspended was Bernice Johnson, later known as Bernice Reagan, whose gut-wrenching voice was the backbone of the female folksinging group Sweet Honey in the Rock. Bernice had been a member of the Albany NAACP's Youth Chapter since her senior year in high school. She had been a member of a delegation that the youth group sent to the white owner of a drugstore in the black community to request that a black clerk be hired. The group failed, but Johnson's spirits weren't dampened. She was in college, and still a member of the NAACP Youth Chapter, when SNCC came to town.

Reagan recalls: "One evening in the fall of 1961, state representatives from the NAACP came to town to tell those of us in the Youth Chapter in Albany that we could not be in SNCC and the NAACP simultaneously. They told us to choose between the two organizations." Bertha Gober voted to go with SNCC that night, but Reagan didn't vote at all.[6]

She didn't make a choice until Gober was arrested trying to implement the ICC ruling. When Reagan joined a campus protest in support of them, she was arrested by Sheriff Laurie Pritchett. She was placed in a crowded, grim jail cell. Here, she not only decided which political path to walk, but developed a "kind of singing that has stuck with me...the kind of singing where the song and the singing are used to say who you are and what you think and to confront and be an instrument for getting through the world."

Gober and Reagan were not the only ones arrested in Albany, Georgia. Before it was all over, Pritchett had packed his city's jails and when there was no more room, farmed out arrested activists to jails in nearby counties. At one point, some fifteen thousand people were behind bars, thanks to Pritchett. Over four hundred high school and college students were arrested when they protested the arrest of eleven SNCC volunteers who tried to integrate the railway terminal. In one jail, eighty-eight women were in one room with twenty steel bunks and no mattresses. "I was in the

Leesburg stockade with 51 other women," one woman recalled later. They would put food in a box, place it on the floor, and kick it into the cell." These were local residents who knew that hundreds of blacks had disappeared into the jails of the Deep South, never to be heard from again. Jail was no laughing matter. Yet they mustered courage, sang freedom songs despite the strong objections of their jailers, and went to jail willingly, in such large numbers, that SNCC historian Howard Zinn wrote, "Never in the nation's history had so many people been imprisoned in one city for exercising the right to protest."[7]

Protests spread to become a city bus boycott when in January 1962, eighteen-year-old Ola Mae Quarterman sat in the front of an Albany city bus and, when told to sit where she was supposed to, snapped back at the white bus driver standing over her, "I paid my damn twenty cents and I can sit where I want." Of course, she was arrested. Still, the Albany Movement protests intensified. Due to the lack of response from Washington, Dr. Martin Luther King, Jr., was called in to help bring national attention to the struggle in this corner of Georgia, some six months later. At this point, Washington did take notice, and King's hasty release defused the bad publicity Albany could have gotten.

Meanwhile, the activists kept the pressure on, with SNCC youngsters seeking access to the city library, lunch counters, Trailways terminal restaurant, the park, the swimming pool, the bowling alley—any and every public facility they could think of. When sixteen-year-old Shirley Gaines tried to get into the bowling alley, she was dragged down stone steps by police officers and kicked again and again in her back and side. Mrs. Marion King, five months pregnant, and carrying a three-year-old child, was knocked unconscious by a deputy sheriff as she brought food to some of the young protesters being held in one of the local jails. A few months later she gave birth to a stillborn child. Still, Mrs. King felt that more good than bad had come out of the Albany movement. Her children had witnessed a courageous

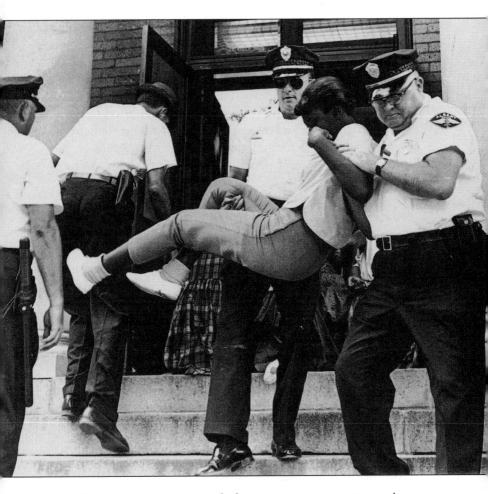

A policeman removes a young girl who is participating in a sit-in at the library in Albany, Georgia.

battle and she thanked the SNCC workers: "You have given my children something that cannot be taken away from them."

SNCC provided funds for local volunteers to apply to their "jail, no bail" strategy, while the NAACP distanced itself from this tactic. Dr. King flew into Albany from time to time to lead marches and to help focus national attention on the town. In it for the long haul, SNCC maintained their effort even though the movement generally looked upon Albany as a defeat. The federal government never once stepped in to enforce federal laws, and Sheriff Pritchett had developed a strategy that caught the movement off guard—there was no violence, no angry white mobs on the street, just pure and unadulterated ain't-no-joke southern jails.

Protests continued through 1963 and 1964. "Finally, the city library was desegregated by court order, though the seats were removed to keep blacks and whites from sitting together. Token integration started in the school system in early 1964, again by judicial demand. And, the city removed all segregation statutes from its books and sold the local swimming pool to a private corporation to avoid the constitutional prohibition against discrimination in public facilities," Zinn reports.

While SNCC and King decided that further protest there would serve no strategic purpose, the lessons of Albany would soon be put to good use in the most segregated city in America—Birmingham, Alabama.

The Birmingham protests presented the world with indelible images of snarling German shepherds attacking schoolchildren. High-powered fire hoses strong enough to rip the bark off trees and tear the skin were unleashed on men, women, and children for all the world to see. Sheriff "Bull" Connor became the quintessential southern sheriff as he brutally led the segregated South's last stand. In places as far away as the Soviet Union, Japan, and China, Birmingham created a highly unflattering image of American democracy. In Albany, Georgia, the Kennedy administration had been able to leave the resolution to local law enforcement officers. In Birmingham, the administration had nowhere to run and nowhere to hide. When Dr. King was jailed and placed in solitary confinement, his wife called

President Kennedy and asked for his help. Before he was released, King published his "Letter from a Birmingham Jail." It gave international attention to the movement by voicing the pain and anguish that had motivated so many thousands throughout the South. Birmingham presented the civil rights movement with its most enduring victory and one of its most heart-wrenching tragedies.

# 9

## FANNIE LOU HAMER
## 1962–1963

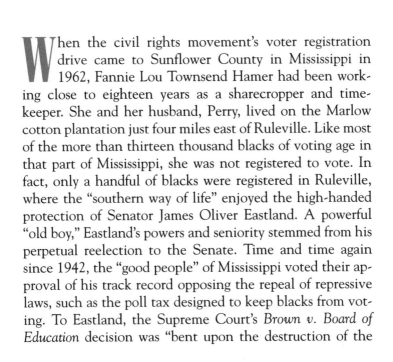

When the civil rights movement's voter registration drive came to Sunflower County in Mississippi in 1962, Fannie Lou Townsend Hamer had been working close to eighteen years as a sharecropper and time-keeper. She and her husband, Perry, lived on the Marlow cotton plantation just four miles east of Ruleville. Like most of the more than thirteen thousand blacks of voting age in that part of Mississippi, she was not registered to vote. In fact, only a handful of blacks were registered in Ruleville, where the "southern way of life" enjoyed the high-handed protection of Senator James Oliver Eastland. A powerful "old boy," Eastland's powers and seniority stemmed from his perpetual reelection to the Senate. Time and time again since 1942, the "good people" of Mississippi voted their approval of his track record opposing the repeal of repressive laws, such as the poll tax designed to keep blacks from voting. To Eastland, the Supreme Court's *Brown v. Board of Education* decision was "bent upon the destruction of the

*Fannie Lou Hamer*

American system of government and the mongrelization of the white race." Blacks were, to Eastland and his ilk, "an inferior race." Eastland was a self-declared "southern reactionary" and damn proud of it, he declared. Later, under Lyndon Johnson's administration, he voted against antipoverty programs, lampooned Mississippi's first Head Start program, and voted against the 1964 Civil Rights Act and the 1965 Voting Rights Act. Eastland was the public face of Sunflower County and as repulsive as he was, he was the milder version of the hatred and fear that lurked in this obscure corner of the country.

Fannie Lou Hamer and other blacks knew the dark side of that kind of racial hatred and its terrorism: lynching, killing, torture, and maiming. This underbelly of the American psyche was so powerful in that part of the country that even by the spring of 1965, after two and a half years of work by civil rights activists, only 155 out of 13,524 black citizens of voting age were registered to vote in Sunflower County; that is 1.1 percent of the population. To stand up to the threats of losing your livelihood and even your life, and of endangering the lives of your family, took guts. Fannie Lou Hamer had guts.

Gory tales of lynchings were told time and time again by blacks and whites in Ruleville. Even when civil rights workers arrived in the area in 1962 they heard these tales told with the spine-tingling, goosebump-provoking details that made it sound as if they had happened only yesterday. And for all its impact, it might as well have. According to one SNCC worker, old women filled with fear and awe would point toward the west and say "Eastland owns this town as far as the eye can see." When mass meetings were held at the Williams Chapel Church, to the displeasure of local whites, all police had to do to scare some folks away was come by with a big police dog in a car, stop black folks on their way to the meetings, and tell them to go home. Many did, but others did not. By mid-August 1962, less than two weeks before Fannie Lou

Hamer would make the trip herself, only three elderly women were willing to go to the courthouse in Indianola to try to register to vote.

Registering to vote in Ruleville, as in the rest of the South, was no easy matter. It was not the simple procedure voters know today: filling out a form, carefully writing your name and address, and waiting to receive your voter registration card in the mail. In the South, for blacks, voter registration was more like an endurance test filled with hurdles, pitfalls, and traps. On August 31, when Hamer and seventeen others took a bus ride to Indianola, they overcame the first hurdle—fear—only to encounter a series of others.

"When we got down there," Hamer recalled, "it was so many people down there, you know, white people and some of them looked like Beverly Hillbillies...but they wasn't kidding around down there; they had on, you know, cowboy hats and they were carrying guns; they had dogs." A hostile circuit court clerk told the blacks that all but two of the seventeen had to leave. Hamer was one of the two he picked to stay. She had to fill out a long questionnaire that asked not only where she lived but for whom she worked. "Well, see, when you put down by whom you were employed, you were fired by the time you get back home," Hamer explained later. Then the registrar asked the potential registrants to interpret a section of the state constitution. As a rule, whites passed, blacks failed. Hamer was asked to interpret the sixteenth section of the Mississippi Constitution dealing with de facto laws. Later she admitted, "I know as much about a facto law as a horse knows about Christmas."[1]

Hamer flunked the test but would keep on trying until she passed. But that day she had to surmount another hurdle—retribution. By the time Hamer got back to Ruleville from Indianola, her boss had already paid her husband a visit and threatened him. That night he came by again to talk to Fannie Lou Hamer directly. He told her to go down to the courthouse and take her name off the registration book. Hamer refused. Of course, she knew what that meant. She was told to take her children and leave the home she had lived in for eighteen years. Her husband, fearing for her life, made her leave town for a while and stay with relatives in a neighboring county. She didn't stay away long. Hamer came back, saying, "Well, killing or no killing, I'm going to stick with civil rights." [2]

And stick she did. Hamer became first an active member of SNCC, then, in 1963, a field secretary. That same year she also finally became a registered voter. But later when Hamer tried to vote in the state's primary election, she was denied the right because she had not been paying poll taxes for two years. Of course, only registered voters paid poll taxes and Hamer had only just registered.

Despite countless roadblocks at every step of the way, Fannie Lou Hamer was a shining example of the down-home, no frills honesty and integrity of a people who had been downtrodden too long. They were determined to change all that, even if it meant making the ultimate sacrifice. Hamer was also a perfect example of what the best of the civil rights movement was about—empowering people to change their own lives.

Getting people to register to vote was one part of a process. Training these people to teach their families, friends, and neighbors to read and take the voter-registration tests was another, as Hamer learned when she attended SCLC's citizenship teacher-training sessions in Dorchester, Georgia. Dorchester was a training school that SCLC had taken over at the urging of Ella Baker when the Tennessee authorities ran the Highlander Folk School out of business. Hamer was so impressive there that she was selected to receive more training at a similar two-week program in Charleston, South Carolina. On her way home from that training session, Hamer experienced her baptism by fire into the civil rights movement.

This was 1963, the most violent year of the civil rights decade. In May, Birmingham's chief of police, Eugene "Bull" Connor, turned his police dogs and fire hoses loose on hundreds of young demonstrators, some as young as nine years old. In June, James Meredith entered the University of Mississippi with the help of NAACP attorneys Thurgood Marshall and Constance Baker Motley and the Justice Department. That same year, Governor George Wallace stood in the school doorway and proclaimed "Segregation today, segregation tomorrow, segregation forever" as he sought to bar black students from integrating the University of Alabama. Nineteen sixty-three was also the year of the March on Washington and the bombing of the Sixteenth Street Baptist Church in Birmingham, Alabama. Things were coming to a head: a storm was sweeping the country, and the South was the eye of the hurricane.

Buses had become the symbol of resistance, thanks to the Montgomery bus boycott, when Hamer and her companions, four other grassroots activists, all women, boarded the bus to return home from Charleston. On June 3, 1963, when the bus made a brief stop in Winona, Mississippi, it was only natural that they would sit down at the lunch counter. It was also only natural that they would be arrested. This was Mississippi, after all, and antisegregation laws simply didn't apply here. When the police officer learned during questioning that Hamer had been at a citizenship training school in Charleston, he interrupted her, "You went to march. You went to see Martin Luther King. We are not going to have it." Handing his blackjack to one of the black inmates, he ordered the man, "I want you to make that bitch wish she was dead." He also threatened the black inmates that if they didn't use the blackjack on her, 'You know what I'll use on you."[3]

According to Hamer, the inmate told her to lie down on the bed. "You mean you would do this to your own race?" she asked him.

"You heard what I said," the policeman yelled.

"So then I had to get over there on the bed flat on my stomach, and the man beat me—that man beat me until he give out." After the other prisoner beat her with a blackjack, Hamer nearly passed out as she got off the cot. But the police officer said, "Hell, you can walk." Four weeks afterward, Hamer still could not sleep on her back. She had been disfigured so badly that she wouldn't let her family see her for a month.

Another member of the group, Arnell Ponder, a coed from Clark College, was beaten by a guard who kept demanding, "Cain't you say yessir, nigger? Cain't you say yessir, bitch?" Ponder, despite being repeatedly slapped, reportedly replied, "Yes, I can say yessir." "Well, say it," the guard ordered. "I don't know you well enough," Ponder retorted.

Hamer heard the sounds from an adjacent cell, and recalled, "She kept screamin' and they kept beatin' her and finally she started prayin' for 'em, and she asked God to have mercy on 'em because they didn't know what they were doin'." When SNCC workers located Ponder and Hamer in jail and got permission to see the prisoners, Ponder's face was so swollen she could barely talk. One SNCC worker reported, "She looked at me and was able to whisper one word: Freedom."[4]

While Hamer's heroism was legendary, it was only indicative of the remarkable courage and determination of women like Arnell Ponder, who dared to join the struggle for change.

At the next SNCC meeting, two factions were battling each other over future strategy: the debate between the need for direct action and the need for voter registration. Each faction saw the two as separate, but through the courage of women like Hamer they would soon be linked.

A coalition, the Council of Federated Organizations (COFO), was formed with all the major civil rights groups: SCLC, SNCC, CORE, and others. All of the civil rights organizations participated in the massive voter registration drive under the umbrella of this group and under the auspices of the national Voter Education Project. The voter registration campaign was called the Mississippi Freedom Summer. Eventually, the drive to register voters would lead to passage of federal legislation, the Voting Rights Act of 1965, which would change the complexion of the country's political leadership.

Before the March on Washington in August 1963 and after Birmingham, direct action seemed to build in intensity as even traditional organizations like the Urban League publicly defended direct action as a strategy and urged blacks to demonstrate and protest. At its annual convention in July, Roy Wilkins urged the NAACP to accelerate, accelerate, accelerate. For the first time the national office provided all-out support for its local branches engaging in direct action, especially in the Carolinas and Mississippi. And, while CORE took the lead in the North, organizing rent strikes and school boycotts, demonstrating against job bias and against police brutality, SNCC and SCLC continued to mount massive voter registration campaigns in Louisiana and Mississippi and to hold massive demonstrations against segregation in Alabama, Florida, Maryland, North and South Carolina, and Virginia. Nineteen sixty-three was the hot year.

The March on Washington was the climax of direct action. Afterward, the movement deemphasized direct action and took up voter registration as its main cause. The leaders expected the passage of the Civil Rights Act to outlaw segregation in public accommodations. The right to vote was the next item on the civil rights agenda. In some areas of the country, as Fannie Lou Hamer could attest, registering to vote was inflammatory and dangerous enough to require tremendous courage.

The potential for black political power in Mississippi, as elsewhere in the "Black Belt," was enormous. Mississippi's 916,000 blacks made up 42 percent of the state's population. A massive effort to register blacks would surely trigger a violent white reaction. No battle on the civil rights front posed greater risks than voter registration in Mississippi. No other campaign required such commitment and courage.

The March on Washington had occurred. Now the direction turned to the voting booth, and while COFO was supposed to be a coalition of SNCC, CORE, NAACP, and others, its next major project, "Mississippi Freedom Summer, 1964," was largely in the hands of SNCC and CORE.

# 10

## FREEDOM SUMMER AND THE MISSISSIPPI FREEDOM DEMOCRATIC PARTY 1964

In 1964, the movement that started when the Supreme Court toppled the separate-but-equal cornerstone of southern segregation shifted its sights from all the niggling signs of Jim Crow—lunch counters, swimming pools, water fountains, waiting rooms in interstate bus terminals— and set out to strike at the racism at the very heart of America's democratic process. Lynchings and other forms of brutality, terrorism, and humiliation to which millions of blacks had been subjected for years, were, after all, an elaborate smoke screen designed to divert attention from the very foundation of the system—the denial of political power. In 1964, the civil rights movement set out to change that and as a result, things would never be the same. The voting booth was the hub linking events in the South with those in the rest of the country, particularly Washington, D.C. Here, it became clear that the South was not some dirty little secret, some skeleton in America's closet; the South was America, and changing the South would inevitably change the entire country.

Ironically, in 1961, several confrontations between freedom riders and segregationists had prompted Attorney General Robert Kennedy to call unsuccessfully for a "cooling-off period," insisting the incidents would embarrass the president during his upcoming meeting with Soviet premier Nikita Khrushchev. Kennedy sought to steer the freedom riders into the less charged territory of voter registration. He even engineered considerable financial support. Little did he know that voter registration would lead to the most confrontational direct action of all—the demand for political empowerment that was at the heart of Freedom Summer, and the Mississippi Freedom Democratic Party's challenge of the electoral process at the 1964 Democratic National Convention.

Freedom Summer, 1964 began as a conscious desire by SNCC organizers to turn up the heat. It grew out of SNCC's successful 1963 Freedom Vote campaign the year before, in which less than one hundred northern white college students helped to register blacks. They held a mock election with an interracial slate of candidates headed by Aaron Henry, president of the Mississippi NAACP; Ed King, Tougalopo College's white chaplain; and Fannie Lou Hamer and Victoria Gray, who ran for congressional seats.

In 1963, of Mississippi's 553,000 African Americans, some 422,256 were eligible to register and vote but only 28,000 had registered. When Fannie Lou Hamer and Victoria Gray were asked by one newspaper journalist why they waged a clearly hopeless campaign, Gray answered: "We feel the time is ripe to begin to let people know that we're serious about this whole thing of becoming first-class citizens. It's not just a sudden burst of energy, we're not going to grow tired and give up. We think our candidacies will have a terrific psychological impact on both races." Gray, ten years younger than Fannie Lou Hamer, had sold cosmetics and household products in Hattiesburg before becoming active in the movement. Like Hamer, she, too, tried repeatedly to register to vote. In fact, the Forrest County registrar didn't decide she had passed the literacy test until the Justice Department filed suit.[1]

At the end of the 1963 Freedom Vote campaign, thousands of black voters had been registered and had voted in the mock election, proving that despite a reign of terror blacks would risk their lives to participate in the democratic process. The Freedom Vote proved a successful mobilizing tool. Now it was time for the real thing.

In June 1964, Fannie Lou Hamer and other civil rights activists traveled to Washington, D.C., to testify at a public hearing led by New York congressman William F. Ryan. They called on the federal government to provide greater protection for civil rights activists. They sent a transcript of their testimony to President Lyndon Baines Johnson and Attorney General Robert F. Kennedy. The government did not respond.

Shortly afterward, three young Freedom Summer volunteers disappeared in Neshoba County, Mississippi, after being arrested by local police on trumped-up traffic charges. The bullet-riddled bodies of James Chaney, an eighteen-year-old SNCC staffer from Meridian, Michael Schwerner, a twenty-five-year-old Brooklyn-born CORE organizer in Meridian, and Andrew Goodman, a twenty-year-old Queens College student summer volunteer, were not found until mid-August, after an extensive search by local and federal authorities. According to one pathologist, James Chaney's badly mutilated body resembled that of an airplane crash victim.

At orientation sessions in Oxford, Ohio, the first leg of their journey, the volunteers were briefed on the task at hand and provided with the skills needed to survive the unique savagery of the Deep South. It would also give them a chance to meet some of the black students who had carried the movement to that point and the remarkable men and women who had been transformed from sharecroppers, teachers, and beauticians into diehard civil rights activists. Throughout the summer, the young white college volunteers would witness and gain respect for the unique strength of those who lived in Mississippi year 'round, the women and men for whom Mississippi was home, not just a summer sojourn, and the fight for freedom, once claimed, was a way of life.

One of those women was Fannie Lou Hamer, who made a strong impression on Sally Belfrage and other volunteers: "Her voice gave everything she had, and her circle soon incorporated the others, expanding first in size and in volume and then something else—it gained passion. Few of them could know who she was, and in her plump, perspiring face many could probably see something of the women who cleaned their mothers' floors at home. But here was clearly someone with force enough for all of them, who knew the meaning of *Oh, Freedom* and *We Shall Not Be Moved* in her flesh and spirit as they never would. They lost their shyness and began to sing the choruses with abandon, though their voices all together faded beside hers."[2]

During an orientation that seemed designed to jolt them with the harsh realization that the South was no ordinary place, and this would be no ordinary summer, they would hear about the challenges of the project from SNCC director James Farmer, who told them simply, "I may be killed. You may be killed." Fannie Lou Hamer on the other hand would give them a sense of their own unique role. One volunteer recalls her saying, "The white man is the scardest person on earth. Out in daylight he don't do nothin'. But at night he'll toss a bomb or pay someone to kill. The white man's afraid he'll be treated like he's been treating the Negroes, but I couldn't carry that much hate. It wouldn't solve any problem for me to hate whites because they hate me. Oh, there's so much hate! Only God has kept the Negro sane.

"Help us communicate with white people. Regardless of what they act like, there's some good there. How can we say we love God and hate our brothers and sisters? We got to reach them."[3] In Hamer, and countless other women the summer volunteers would witness a unique combination of fierce determination to win first-class citizenship, "redemptive forgiveness," and an overwhelming warmth as these women took the white students into their homes. The recollections of hundreds of summer volunteers, interviewed by Doug McAdam for his insightful book, *Freedom Summer*, are sprinkled with stories of the kindness of rank-and-file black women in the movement, such as Hamer. Despite the fact that "sheltering the 'invaders' was grounds for harassment, dismissal from a job, or worse," they were treated like members of the family and even protected by the women who took them in. One recalled, "I am writing this at 6 A.M. Just now coming down the hall from the bathroom, I met Mrs. Fairley coming down that hall from the front porch carrying a rifle in one hand and a pistol in the other. I do not know what is going on. [All she said was,] 'You go to sleep, let me fight for you.'[4]

Another said her life had changed, after the first night of orientation in Oxford, "because I met those SNCC people and my mouth fell open."

Novices and veterans working together on the project would witness a sea change both in themselves and their country as they undertook the task at hand.

Every step of the way, women played instrumental roles, sometimes providing the moral force that kept other activists true to their ideals, sometimes being the lightning rod that galvanized national attention to their cause. Sometimes they were the ones to reveal the class, caste, and sexist riffs within the movement itself.

The project's locations were chosen for tactical reasons. Voter registration, freedom schools, and community centers were set up in thirty-two principal projects located in all five of Mississippi's congressional districts.

SNCC field secretary Charlie Cobb was credited with being the chief architect of the Freedom Schools, with Staughton Lynd, a Spellman history professor, serving as the director of this facet of the project, according to chronicler McAdams. But the concept was by no means new. What many historians of the movement have ignored is the role women played in developing the freedom, or citizenship, schools and making them an instrumental component of the civil rights movement.

Two women who helped establish citizenship schools as a key segment of the struggle were Septima Poinsette Clark and Dorothy Cotton. Clark's career as director of education and teaching for the Southern Christian Leadership Conference began when Myles Horton, director of the Highlander Folk School, asked her to come run his workshops. Clark had lost her teaching job in South Carolina because of her involvement with the NAACP. She helped develop the Highlander's Citizenship Education Program with its dual thrust of political empowerment and literacy training. "Myles thought we could just go into communities and get people registered to vote," Clark said. But she knew folks had to be trained to read their state's constitutions in order to attempt to answer the difficult questions registrars often asked blacks.[5]

The effectiveness of the training offered in these citizenship schools is obvious from the roster of the women who passed through their doors—Rosa Parks, Fannie Lou Hamer, and Ella Baker, to name a few.

Clark recalls Rosa Parks as a quiet, timid woman who, when asked what she planned to do upon returning home, said, "Montgomery was the cradle of the confederacy and nothing would happen there because blacks wouldn't stick together."[6] That was three months before the Montgomery bus boycott.

Soon after Ella Baker worked with Clark at Highlander, Clark was recruited to join SCLC's staff. Baker had often urged Dr. Martin Luther King, Jr., to stress citizenship education in order to develop grassroots leaders. When he decided to take her advice, he asked Myles Horton to develop a program for SCLC. Horton apparently suggested that SCLC take over Highlander.

Dorothy Cotton joined SCLC's staff when, in 1963,

*A session at the Highlander Folk School. Rosa Parks is seated at center.*

King recruited her mentor, Wyatt T. Walker, to become SCLC's executive director. Cotton became director of SCLC's Citizenship Education Program, and SCLC took over the Highlander Folk School program when Horton closed the school after enduring years of harassment by Tennessee authorities. Together with Andrew Young, Septima Clark and Dorothy Cotton traveled across the South recruiting participants for the training program. One of the people they trained was Fannie Lou Hamer, who Cotton rememberd as the dynamic personality in the Mississippi group.

Clark also had strong feelings about how women in the movement were treated: "I was on the executive staff of SCLC, but the men on it didn't listen to me too well. They liked to send me into many places because I could always make a path in to get people to listen to what I have to say. But those men didn't have any faith in women, whatsoever. They just thought women were sex symbols and had no contribution to make."[7]

The Freedom Schools, were successful long before Freedom Summer 1964. In 1962, there were forty citizenship schools in South Carolina. By 1964 there were eighty, and the black voting strength increased from 57,000 to 150,000. In southeast Georgia in 1964, there were thirty citizenship schools in seven counties. So in many ways, it was on the tradition of Highlander that Cotton and Clark and the Freedom Summer volunteers were building when they opened their own Freedom Schools.

Voter registration was the other important task of Freedom Summer 1964. At the beginning of the summer, black voters in the state constituted 6.7 percent of Mississippi's registered voters, the lowest of any state in the union. Nineteen sixty-four was a presidential election year. SNCC organizers had decided that since blacks in Mississippi were locked out of the Democratic party, they would create their own, the Mississippi Freedom Democratic party (MFDP). They were very methodical. First, they ran a slate of candidates for a Senate seat and three House seats in the June Democratic primary. When these candidates were defeated, and their attempt to be placed on the ballot as independents was stymied by the state board of elections, SNCC leaders decided to hold their own "mock" election to challenge the Mississippi delegates to the August Democratic National Convention in Atlantic City, New Jersey.

They registered eighty thousand prospective voters and

held a state convention in Jackson on August 6, where sixty-eight people were chosen to represent them at the Democratic National Convention. Ella Baker gave the convention's keynote address, described as a passionate promise that, whether recognized at Atlantic City or not, the MFDP, would grow to be a powerful political arm of the movement in Mississippi.

Among the MFDP delegates who journeyed to Atlantic City in the late summer of 1964 were Ella Baker, Fannie Lou Hamer, Annie Devine, Victoria Gray, Eleanor Holmes Norton, and Marian Wright Edelman. Once in Atlantic City, they found themselves smack dab in the middle of the traditional hardball, wheeling-and-dealing political arena. Heavy-handed wrangling surrounded the MFDP's challenge. The women endured snubs from men in their own delegation. Against them were black political and civil rights leaders who were dependent on the forces arrayed against the MFDP for patronage and support. Still, they held their ground. One of the Democratic convention's most memorable highlights was Fannie Lou Hamer's testimony before the credentials committee. She told them of her repeated attempts to register to vote, her beating in the Winona jail, and more, before ending with tears streaming down her face, "All of this on account we want to register to become first-class citizens. And if the Freedom Democratic Party is not seated, I question America. Is this America, the land of the free and the home of the brave, where we have to sleep with our telephones off the hooks because our lives be threatened daily because we want to live as decent human beings, in America?" Her words even brought tears to the eyes of hard-bitten, seasoned politicians. But President Lyndon Johnson, determined not to have his convention marred, pulled the plug on her testimony with a hastily called press conference. In spite of these shenanigans, word got out when Hamer's speech was later rebroadcast on nationwide television. The MFDP also found itself the target of hostility from black delegates angry at them for daring to rock the boat. At one point, an angry Roy Wilkins, head of the NAACP, cornered Fannie Lou Hamer, lashing out at her for not accepting the compromise crafted by party leaders. The MFDP was offered two at-large seats for their sixty-eight-member delegation. According to Hamer, Wilkins said, "You people have put your point across. You don't know anything, you're ignorant, you don't know anything about politics. I have been in the business over 20 years. You people have put your point across, now why don't you pack up and go home?" Even the men in their delegation wanted to settle, but the women took a strong stand. With impassioned pleas and a little arm-twisting, the group finally voted 60 to 4 against the compromise. Fannie Lou Hamer later told the press, "We didn't come all this way for no two seats."

While the MFDP walked away empty-handed, it had more of an impact than even the delegates imagined at the time. The MFDP challenged the seating of the five segregationist members in June 1965 at the opening of Congress, and though they lost, the 149 representatives voting in their favor was a considerable display of support. The MFDP continued running candidates, and in 1967 twenty-two African Americans were elected to office in Mississippi, the most since Reconstruction.

Beginning in 1968, the Rules Committee of the Democratic Party refused to seat any delegation that had been constituted through racially discriminatory means. Also, beginning in 1972, the party added a restriction barring any delegation that failed to meet a gender quota for delegation membership. While the MFDP led a somewhat shaky existance through the mid-1970s, its challenge opened up the national conventions to more blacks, women, Latinos, and Asian Americans than ever before.

When Freedom Summer 1964 was over, it was clear that much had changed. The SNCC activists came out of it taking a new look at everything, from the value of electoral politics and working with the traditional two-party structure to the relationship between women and men and blacks and whites in the movement. The summer of 1964 exposed fault lines in America that would lead to social tremors. These would erupt in the earthquakes called the women's liberation movement, the New Left, the gay liberation struggle, and more. Freedom Summer was, in many ways, the culmination of the civil rights movement and a sign of its transformation into something bigger, broader, and perhaps better.

The movement officially crossed a bridge in 1965 when marchers headed from Selma, Alabama, to Montgomery were stopped by state troopers, clubbed and gassed as they knelt to pray. The world looked on in horror and outrage. President Lyndon Baines Johnson proposed the Voting Rights Act of 1965. Afterward, the focus of the African-American struggle for equality shifted from the South to the North, from peaceful nonviolence to Black Power "by any means necessary." Riots broke out in Watts, Harlem, Detroit, and other major northern cities.

With this transformation, the struggles within the civil rights movement also erupted as women moved to demand equal respect and leadership. Women like Fran M. Beals, New York coordinator of the SNCC Black Women's Liberation Committee, exposed the "double jeopardy" of being black and female within the liberation movement. Beals bluntly called the black woman "the slave of a slave," as she called for an end to second-class citizenship within the movement.

Beals's voice might have represented the voices of countless young women crossing the bridge from the civil rights movement onto the next wave of struggles, but many veterans shared these sentiments. For far too long their contributions were downplayed and overlooked. Yet, where would the movement have been without them? Septima Clark was right when she said that the work the women did during the time of civil rights is what really carried the movement along. The women carried forth the ideas. The civil rights movement would never have taken off if some women hadn't started to speak up.

# SOURCE NOTES

## CHAPTER 1

1. Gloria Richardson Dandridge, interview, 1994.
2. Gloria Richardson Dandridge, interview, 1994.
3. Gerda Lerner, ed., *Black Women in White America: A Documentary History*. New York: Pantheon Books, 1972., p. 596.
4. Brian Lanker, *I Dream a World: Portraits of Black Women Who Changed America*. New York: Stewart, Tabori & Chang, 1989, p. 74.
5. Juan Williams, *Eyes on the Prize: America's Civil Rights Years, 1954-1965*. New York: Penguin Books, 1987, p. 25.
6. Jack Greenberg, *Crusaders in the Courts: How a Dedicated Band of Lawyers Fought for the Civil Rights Movement*. New York: Basic Books/HarperCollins Publishers, Inc., 1994, p. 39.
7. Constance Baker Motley, "My Personal Debt to Thurgood Marshall," *Yale Law Journal*, November 1991.
8. Marian Wright Edelman, *Lady Lawyer*. New York: Farrar Straus Giroux, 1986, p. 42.
9. Lanker, p. 73.
10. Williams, p. 130.
11. Charlayne Hunter-Gault, *In My Place*. New York: Farrar Straus Giroux, 1992, p. 121.
12. Lerner, p. 1034.
13. Angela Davis, interview, 1994.

## CHAPTER 3

1. All information in this chapter is from the author's interview with Esther Cooper and James Jackson 1995.

## CHAPTER 4

1. Greenberg, p. 38.
2. Williams, p. 15.
3. All Eckford quotes from Daisy Bates, *The Long Shadow of Little Rock, A Memoir*. New York, David McKay Co., 1962, p. 30.
4. Beals quotes from Williams, p. 108.
5. Bates, p. 42.
6. Williams, p. 80.
7. All quotes from Hunter-Gault.

## CHAPTER 5

1. Jo Ann Robinson's account is taken from the book by David J. Garrow and Jo Ann Robinson, *The Montgomery Bus Boycott and the Women Who Started It*. Knoxville: University of Tennessee, 1987.
2. Ibid., p. 37.
3. Ibid., p. 39.
4. Ibid., p. 18.
5. Ibid., p. 37.
6. Ibid., p. 39.
7. Ibid., p. 20.
8. Ibid., p. 20.
9. Ibid., p. 42.
10. Ibid., p. 43.

## CHAPTER 6

1. Giddings, p. 267.
2. Harvard Sitkoff, *The Struggle for Black Equality, 1954-1980*. New York: Hill and Wang, 1981, p. 72.
3. Howard Zinn, *SNCC: Student Nonviolent Coordinating Committee, The New Abolitionists*. Boston: Beacon Press, 1979, p. 16.
4. Ibid., p. 17.
5. Ibid., p. 19.
6. Ibid., p. 20.
7. Williams, p. 120.
8. Ella Baker, "More Than a Hamburger." From *The Eyes on the Prize Reader*, ed. Clayborne Carson, David J. Garrow, Gerald Gill, Vincent Harding, and Darlene Clark Hine. New York: Penguin Books, 1991, p. 120.
9. Ibid, p. 122.
10. Cantarow and O'Malley, p. 234.
11. Carson et al., p. 148.
13. Giddings, p. 278.

## CHAPTER 7

1. Giddings, p. 278.
2. Ibid., p. 279.
3. Sitkoff, p. 97.
4. Giddings, p. 280.
5. Williams, p. 149.
6. Zinn, p. 57.

## CHAPTER 8

1. Giddings, p. 285.
2. Ibid., p. 285.
3. The Richardson Dandrige quotes are from author's interview, 1994. Also see Annette K. Brock, "Gloria Richardson and the Cambridge Movement," *Women in the Civil Rights movement, Trailblazers and Torchbearers,* 1941-1965. ed. Vicki L. Crawford, Jacqueline Anne Rouse, and Barbara Woods (1990).
4. Zinn, p. 123.
5. Zinn, p. 125.
6. Bernice Reagan and Sweet Honey in the Rock. *We Who Believe in Freedom.* New York: Anchor Books/Doubleday, 1993, p. 153.
7. Zinn, p. 131.

## CHAPTER 9

1. Kay Mills, *This Little Light of Mine: The Life of Fannie Lou Hamer.* New York: Dutton, 1993, p. 17.
2. Ibid., p. 45
3. Ibid., p. 46.
4. Ibid., p. 48.

## CHAPTER 10

1. Mills, p. 94.
2. Sally Belfrage, *Freedom Summer.* Charlottesville: University Press of Virginia, 1990, p. 48.
3. Ibid., p. 48.
4. Ibid., p. 50.
5. Septima Clark, p. 52.
6. Septima Clark, p. 33.
7. Dorothy Cotton, "Literacy and Liberation." In *Freedomways,* 1946. p. 113.

# INDEX